D1451231

SURFERS SOULIES SKINHEADS & SKATERS

SUBCULTURAL STYLE FROM THE FORTIES TO THE NINETIES

SURFERS SOULIES SKINHEADS & SKATERS

SUBCULTURAL STYLE FROM THE FORTIES TO THE NINETIES

AMY DE LA HAYE AND CATHIE DINGWALL
PHOTOGRAPHY BY DANIEL McGRATH

The Overlook Press
Woodstock • New York

First published in the United States in 1996 by

The Overlook Press
Lewis Hollow Road
Woodstock, New York 12498

De la Haye, Amy.
Surfers soulies skinheads & skaters:
street styles from the forties to the nineties
Amy de la Haye, Cathie Dingwall; photography by Danny McGrath.
p. cm.
Includes bibliographical references and index.
1. Costume - History - 20th century.
2. Fashion - History - 20th century.
3. Subculture - History - 20th century.
I. Dingwall, Cathie. II. Title.
GT596.D43 1996
391'.009 - dc20
96-18132
ISBN: 0-87951-689-5
Designed by johnson banks
Printed in Singapore by C.S. Graphics

Frontispiece: Punk, Modzart, UK, printed cotton trousers 1977
(Given by John and Molly Dove, Modzart)

First American Edition

INTRODUCTION

From the Cowboy's embroidered shirt and the flowing robes of 1960s Hippies to the sharp suits of Teddy Boys, the layered garb of eco-friendly Travellers and the futuristic fantasies of Cyberpunk, youth subcultures have flourished and have often inspired high fashion.

Between 1992 and 1994 Amy de la Haye and Cathie Dingwall acquired for the V&A's Textiles and Dress Department a unique collection of authentic subcultural clothes worn from the 1940s to the 1990s, which were displayed in an exhibition which opened in November 1994. V&A photographer Daniel McGrath took the stunning full-length and detail photographs.

Unlike other publications, which explore the multi-faceted nature of subcultural identity, this book is object based. The focus is upon clothing worn by individuals to signify their allegiance to a particular subculture. That is, it concentrates upon 'real clothes' worn by 'real people', complete with all the individual nuances that this approach embraces. Each photograph is accompanied by a detailed caption identifying the source of the garments and, where possible, including a personal statement from the wearer or fashion designer.

The first part describes the nature of subcultural style, explores the relationship between high fashion and 'the street' and explains how the clothing was collected. The concluding essay considers subcultures within a theoretical framework and analyses the implications of collecting and displaying objects that, by definition, reject the prevailing ethos within a national museum which is primarily devoted to the decorative arts.

SUBCULTURES AND STYLE

Membership of subcultural groups, whose ideas and lifestyles are at variance with those of the dominant culture, is usually dominated by the young. For some it is fleeting and forms a rite of passage; others move through a series of subcultures, and some remain committed to one, long term. Belonging to a subculture can be liberating, offering, for example, certain freedoms in lifestyle, sexuality and politics. By defining their own geographical, social and sartorial boundaries, subcultures also provide a sense of belonging which is independent of the family. Style is central to subcultural identity, and clothing and body adornment are the most visible emblems of membership signifying loyalty to kindred spirits and exclusion to the world at large.

In the past, alternative forms of dressing were adopted by, among others, the Incroyables and Pre-Raphaelites, as well as members of the Bloomsbury Group. They adopted what were popularly considered as outlandish clothes to make personal, aesthetic or political statements. A defiant rejection of the prevailing fashion was to risk widespread ridicule and even social ostracism. Such an anti-fashion stance was, therefore, generally the privilege of the aristocracy and of artists, literary and crafts people, who could afford to flaunt their rebellious attitudes through their modes of dress. Since the watershed of the Second World War there have been significant cultural shifts, and alternative dressing is no longer the preserve of an elite.

Post-war subcultures emerged partly in response to full employment and increased levels of youth affluence. They were also a product of the changing social landscape in which young, often working-class youth had the confidence to adopt styles which were different from those chosen by their parents and to deviate from fashion's dictates. Music, rather than art, politics or literature, was the primary fuel for post-war subcultures, and many emerged in tandem with new forms of musical expression. Traditionally, musicians personified subcultural styles, but perhaps this is less true in the 1990s, with young, innovative, clothing designers eclipsing their lead.

Small specialist retailers, tailors, markets and mail-order catalogues predominantly serve the demand for subcultural clothing, along with selected large-scale manufacturers whose product is deemed 'authentic'. These companies include Dr Martens, Fred Perry and Levi's, which were founded to supply the need for utilitarian or sports clothes, as opposed to a fashion market. Once their goods are appropriated by a subculture, the meanings of the clothes are transformed – the Skinheads' laced working boot and the Punks' use of safety-pins provide well-known examples.

Within the stylistic boundaries of subcultures there is much emphasis upon personal expression and many clothes are home-made. Items bought in the high street are often customized and this takes many forms, including crudely distressing denim jeans, emblazoning denim and leather jackets with badges, patches and painted decoration and intricately embroidering embellishments. The second-hand clothes market also dresses many subcultural members, reflecting both the precarious financial position of many young people and a passion for authentic retro clothes.

SUBCULTURAL STYLE AND HIGH FASHION

It is perhaps ironic that subcultural styles – which have so often emerged as an iconoclastic alternative to high fashion – have come to exert such a dominant stylistic influence upon it, especially during the first half of the 1990s. The energy and authenticity associated with 'the street' have become highly desirable, and fashion designers are not alone in seeking to exploit these valuable qualities. Fashion's focus is, of course, upon clothing and adornment, rather than rooted in ideas and lifestyles.

There are several established routes by which high fashion designs trickle down to influence what is available in the high street. Some are officially sanctioned, such as the purchase of toiles, and then there is much illegal piracy. Magazines, newspapers, videos and professional fashion forecasting agencies also feed into the dissemination process. Today the call for design protection is no longer exclusive to top fashion designers. Many designers serving subcultural and streetstyle markets now see adaptations of their own creations celebrated – and occasionally copied – on the international catwalks. However, rarely is the version a literal copy. Most fashion designers incorporate elements from the street into their own distinctive styles, which, combined with luxurious fabrics and quality workmanship, creates a look that is unique and does not attempt to be subcultural.

As chief designer at the house of Christian Dior, Yves Saint Laurent was possibly the first high fashion designer to recognize the stylistic charge of the street. His 1960 interpretations of the Rockers' leather jackets, in mink-trimmed crocodile skin with matching helmet-style millinery, were launched upon a fashion world not yet ready to recognize subcultural references, however luxurious. Opening his own house in 1962, Yves Saint Laurent continued to look to the street, this time to the existentialists centred around Paris's Left Bank.

Throughout the 1960s and 1970s there were echoes of the street on the catwalk: Mary Quant picked up on Mod styles, Bill Gibb drew on the Hippy love of kaftans, and in 1977 Zandra Rhodes presented her Punk-inspired Conceptual Chic collection, which featured silk jersey sheath dresses, decorated with jewelled safety-pins holding together beautifully finished holes and slashes. Since the early 1990s, fashion designers have not just drawn upon one or two subcultural styles, but have extracted elements from many subcultures to use in a single collection. In true postmodern style these are freely combined with historical, cross-cultural and futuristic influences to create new fashions.

The high fashion designers involved in the Streetstyle Exhibition were invited to participate in an area where they acknowledged stylistic inspiration. Some had kept items from previous collections, while others generously re-made pieces from original fabrics and patterns. Many of the captions that accompany the photographs of high fashion include statements from the designers about their use of subcultural references.

The dissemination of design is not just a two-way process; it is also cyclical. Far from rejecting high fashion, some of the more recent subcultures have wholeheartedly basked in the status given by top designer labels. In the 1980s, Casuals went to great lengths to obtain clothing by Burberry and Ralph Lauren. In more recent years, Louis Vuitton and Gucci accessories have represented the ultimate to B-Boys, and the Chanel look is central to many Ragga girls. Blatantly labelled, original designer clothing – ideally by Italian designers Moschino, Versace and Armani – forms the core of young, black, 1990s Junglists' style. While in all cases the original label is most coveted, fakes are often the reality. Rarely are such replicas convincing, but none the less they have the superficial cachet of association.

STREETSTYLE CLOTHING

'Streetstyle' often describes the adornments and clothing of the material culture of subcultures. It also, and perhaps more appropriately, embraces individual, generally youthful, expressions of style that do not emanate from the catwalk, but are without subcultural commitment. Streetstyle is often an entirely personal statement, resulting in a look that defies classification and which can change from day to day. This sartorial freedom has been particularly celebrated since the early 1980s, and the profile of streetstyle designers has been significantly raised. The introduction of the *style* magazines *The Face* and *iD* can take much of the credit. Founded in 1980, they have acted as trailblazers, saluting and publicizing the work of streetstyle designers as well as celebrating the style statements of the individual. In 1995 the British Fashion Awards formally acknowledged the special significance of streetstyle to British fashion by launching a new Streetstyle category. Sign of the Times, Hussein Chalayan and Red or Dead were nominated, with the last winning.

The selection of streetstyle outfits shown in this book reveals just a few of the multiplicity of pluralistic looks available during 1993 and 1994. The choice was phenomenal, and we decided to focus upon those which drew upon past and present subcultural styles. The captions reveal which subcultures have influenced the outfits.

SUBCULTURAL STYLE TODAY

Since the early 1990s the stylistic boundaries between subcultures and high fashion have become blurred. While racial, sexual and lifestyle tensions between the groups continue to exist, the one new and extremely significant development is that for the first time certain subcultures occupy some common ground. In clubs such as London's Megadog, and at such festivals as Glastonbury, Travellers, Ravers and many other subcultural hybrids share the same space because the music, ambience and general attitude bring them together.

Individuals and magazine stylists now freely mix clothing from the big names of high fashion with items from fledgling streetstyle designers to create clothes that have subcultural associations and period pieces to represent the current vogue for eclecticism. However, distinctive subcultures do still exist, as the die-hard Teddy Boys, Skinheads and Hippies and young revivalists seen on the streets today testify. There is also a host of new subcultures, such as New Age, Technos, Bhangra, Ragga and Junglists each with their own ideas, ethnicity and style.

SUBCULTURAL STYLE AT THE V&A

The V&A's collection policy for 20th-century dress converges upon cutting-edge design. Traditionally, the criterion for selection demanded the most luxurious, *haute-couture* and exclusive levels of ready-to-wear clothing, which emanated from the gilded salons of top international fashion designers. In the light of recent developments, we decided to broaden our scope to embrace subcultural clothing, acknowledging its significance as a stylistic force and as a national, cultural expression.

Since 1992, impelled by the momentum and concentration of preparing for an exhibition, we started actively to collect subcultural clothes from the 1940s to the present day. As well as British styles, crucial Caribbean and American developments are also pinpointed. Within each category the aim was to acquire examples of original and revival styles, as well as clothes worn by both sexes. (And, in the case of New Age Travellers, a baby too!). The Textiles and Dress Department now houses some 125 subcultural outfits, which we will continue to build upon, filling in gaps as well as adding new styles as they emerge. We are thus committed to a dual policy of collecting examples of authentic subcultural outfits, with examples of high fashion 'spin-offs', and continuing our traditional emphasis upon the exclusive designs of international fashion houses.

The acquisition of subcultural clothes, accompanied by oral testimony and on occasion snapshots of the donor wearing the clothes, depended upon the support of a great many people who acted as consultants and advisors, and who provided vital introductions. To these we are deeply indebted. Many worked in a voluntary capacity, driven by a passion for the accurate representation of the subculture to which they belonged and for the formation of a unique collection of clothes. Some are personally mentioned at the end of this section, but to everyone involved we reiterate our immense gratitude. The acquisition of each outfit has a story to tell, and the following examples illustrate some of the varied means by which just a few were discovered.

Patricia Essam (neé Goodman) in 1954 (on the left)

Patricia Essam in 1994, with snapshots of herself as a Teddy Girl in 1954

As one of our key consultants, Judy Westacott was instrumental in obtaining a number of outfits, especially for the Teddy Boy, Rocker and Rockabilly sections with which she had personal involvement. Some of the clothes exhibited were her own, while others belonged to friends and acquaintances. Judy is fastidious about obtaining original subcultural authenticity. She has researched extensively into the histories of these subcultures and provided detailed contextual information about each. Her commitment to the project became a labour of love. To our delight, she regularly appeared on her bike or in a van with head-to-toe outfits and detailed information about each. However, the one item she was unable to obtain for the exhibition was an original 1950s Teddy Boy or Teddy Girl jacket. Owners of these rare and cherished items could not be persuaded to part with them, even on a temporary loan basis for the duration of the exhibition. Via the Museum's Press Office we approached the BBC *Clothes Show* to ask if they would put out an appeal on national television. As a result, we obtained a 1950s Teddy Boy waistcoat, three 1960s Teddy Boy jackets, a pair of blue suede shoes and, ultimately, a letter from Mrs Patricia Essam with a snapshot of herself wearing her prized Teddy Girl jacket in 1954, which she had kept wrapped in tissue for 40 years. A trip to Milton Keynes to meet Pat led to the successful acquisition of the jacket, which she had had made-to-measure by Weaver to Wearer in Northhampton, complete with oral testimony and copies of her snapshots. During the day she often wore the jacket with tartan trousers and 'lace-up-the-leg' sandals and for evening with a long black pencil skirt and stiletto heeled shoes. Her black wool draped jacket, with matching velvet trim, looks pretty innocuous today, but in describing the shock and even hostility aroused when she wore it, she emphasized the power of subcultural clothes to shake the status quo in 1950s Britain.

Carol Tulloch worked with us in acquiring a number of the black subcultural clothes and also generously shared her extensive research with us. Together we visited markets and shops in Brixton and Dalston and made a number of useful contacts. We also met Derek and his daughter Esther Falconer who run a specialist period shop called Crazy Clothes in Ladbroke Grove, West London. Derek came to Britain from the Caribbean in the 1950s, has always worked in clothing trades and has a labyrinth of contacts. He obtained authentic Rasta clothes, complete with bongs, Yardie and Funk outfits, in addition to parting with his own brown leather Soul Boy outfit.

Keith Mallinson with the
pattern for the Northern
Soul trousers 1994

The 1970s Northern Soul suit was obtained after Marion Hume, fashion editor of *The Independent*, appealed to her readers. In response, Peter Davies contacted us to see if we were interested in his 1975 grey suit jacket, with the characteristic multiple pockets. In common with many people, he had retained the jacket but had had his trousers altered with the passage of time. He suggested we approach Keith Mallinson, the Rotherham-based tailor who originally made the suit, to see if he had kept his patterns for the requisite 40-inch flared trousers. Fortunately Keith had and rose to the challenge of finding matching fabric and re-creating the missing trousers. This was the only instance where trousers were re-created, because the tailors who had made other missing items were no longer in business, and thus the jackets are shown alone.

The New Age Traveller clothes were obtained by Sarah Callard who worked fulltime on the project for two years. She visited members of the Dongas tribe and invited them to participate in the project. The Dongas tribe, who live in and around the Forest of Dean, choose an alternative lifestyle based on travelling, subsistence and on promoting environmental issues. They largely reject mainstream consumerist values and live in a way which creates a minimum impact upon the environment. Fraggle (an assumed name) parted with one of her multi-layered, colourful outfits, complete with the wooden crochet hook and spoon she had carved, and the licorice stick used to clean her teeth, all of which were worn on thongs around her neck. Communication with Fraggle and her colleagues depended upon Sarah making several visits to the Forest of Dean and their phoning the V&A from public call boxes.

It was not possible in all cases to obtain complete head-to-toe outfits from one person. Where such items as boots were missing, suitably worn replacements were sought. The captions clearly state whether the clothes photographed were 'worn by' or 'compiled by' someone. The compiled outfits were put together by people who had not kept their own clothes, but felt that they could successfully re-create the attire they or their friends had once worn. Lou Taylor went to great lengths to re-create an outfit she had worn during the late 1950s and early 1960s by scouring army surplus and second-hand clothing shops throughout England and Scotland. Lou was active in the Youth Campaign for Nuclear Disarmament. In contrast to the extremely feminine, fully accessorized and highly made-up fashion of the day, Lou and her fellow students adopted cheap and practical, often army surplus, clothes and flat lace up shoes for active campaigning.

In four instances, after searching long and hard, we decided to have replicas made of significant items - again this is clearly stated on the accompanying captions. Extensive research, appeals in national newspapers, radio and television failed to unearth an original 1940s Zoot Suit, and it was crucial that this early, flamboyant, Afro-Caribbean American subculture be represented. This style enjoyed a revival, spearheaded by bands such as Kid Creole and Blue Rondo a la Terk, during the early 1980s. We approached Chris Sullivan, lead singer of Blue Rondo a la Terk, who had worn meticulous re-creations of this look, to design a replica for us. His drawing was based on his own researches, which included a detailed study of the clothes worn in the cult 1943 film *Stormy Weather*. Chris then introduced us to his tailor, Chris Ruocco, who made up the suit in a pale green wool and also made the shirt and characteristic exaggerated bow tie. This is teamed with original 1940s pale green leather braces and co-respondent shoes from the Textiles and Dress Collection.

Clothing representing the most recent subcultures was usually obtained by approaching shops and designers in the first instance. Outfits were either acquired directly from the shop owners or designers or via their friends and contacts. Sometimes the people involved were well known, such as Normski, who provided much help and clothing for the B-Boy section. Most of the clothes shown in this book now form part of the permanent collection of the Textiles and Dress Department, although some items were on loan for the exhibition and these are identified on the captions.

As in the exhibition, the clothes in this book are consciously presented devoid of contextual settings. We felt that such props would be inappropriate as they would detract from the clothing and were beyond our scope. Clearly conventional fashion mannequins would have been wrong for the display of subcultural clothes. We wanted dress forms without pronounced gender or racial features and which did not celebrate 'supermodel' beauty. The customized flatbacks, commissioned from Universal Display Limited, accommodated the display of clothes of all sizes and the adjustable leg poles ensured that each figure assumed the height of the original wearer.

Body adornments, hairstyles and cosmetics are all crucial elements of subcultural style, but it was beyond our scope to attempt to re -create them. We also felt that photographic portraits could authentically reveal these to exhibition visitors and could provide companion volumes to our readers. Thus, distressed metal heads were designed by V&A designer Sharon Beard, to provide necessary proportion and support hats and sun-glasses. Curators and professional stylists created the initial ensembles and then wearers were invited to make adjustments and provide finishing touches before press or public were admitted to the exhibition. These photographs were taken just before the exhibition was dismantled. The clothes are now kept in the Textiles and Dress reference collection and can be viewed by appointment.

GLOSSARY Compiled by Sarah Callard and Will Hoon

This glossary has been written to explain terms and phrases used throughout the book. The whole concept of streetstyle depends upon the fact that it remains marginalized and, to an extent, elitist. Along with the clothing there is, of course, a whole range of streetstyle ephemera such as music, cars or motorbikes. Often there is a different kind of language too which helps to maintain the esoteric and subversive atmosphere surrounding a youth cult, and makes it attractive to young people. Growing out of various streetstyles, many of the phrases explained in this glossary were invented by the media in order to categorize and report on specific movements.

AFROCENTRIC Describes a movement amongst Black Americans proudly promoting their race, culture and roots. It was made popular by bands such as Arrested Development, Jungle Brothers and A Tribe Called Quest in the late 1980s. African pendants, denoting an inter-ethnic African culture, replaced the chunky gold jewellery which was a stalwart of B-Boy dress (probably imported from South Africa).

B-BOY The name given to young, urban Black Americans associated with the Rap and Hip-Hop scene. The prefix 'B' has a variety of explanations; bad, break and beat have all been suggested as possible interpretations. The name came into common usage in Britain during the late 1980s through hit singles by the Beastie Boys and Run DMC. Although there are many looks associated with the term, one of the most definitive consisted of labelled sports clothes, specific brands of trainers, baseball caps and chunky (often gold) jewellery.

BEATNIK The name given to young jazz-loving bohemians of 1950s San Francisco, New York and London. The name and inspiration were drawn from the American 'beat poets' exemplified by writers such as Jack Kerouac and Allen Ginsberg. Beatniks were also heavily influenced by French existentialist writers and the ideas of a young radical avant-garde. 'Beats' often appropriated the language of black jazz musicians, the utilitarian clothing of workmen and the lifestyle of radical intellectuals.

BHANGRA A style of music and dress popular amongst Asian youths since the late 1970s, which fuses the traditional with the contemporary. The dress style associated with Bhangra music combines traditional Indian clothing with contemporary Western sports and casual wear.

CARIBBEAN Designates the style of dress worn by West Indians who migrated to Britain in the 1950s. This tended to be unique tailor-made clothing, using light, brightly coloured fabrics.

CASUALS Describes late 1970s/early 1980s British football gangs. The name was coined to emphasize their chosen gangwear of European designer leisurewear and branded sports clothes.

CYBERPUNK Punk styles meet science fiction in virtual reality. Inspired by the apocalyptic films *Mad Max* (*1*, *2* and *3*) and *Bladerunner*, as well as the new genre of adult comics, Cyberpunk combines futuristic fantasy and techno-fetishism. Advances in computer technology have opened up the world of electronic intelligence to a host of subversive cliques and cults, prompted by a new underground dedicated to 'playing' in cyberspace. The style adopted by people calling themselves Cyberpunks might consist of black leather, rubber and PVC, mixed with industrial-looking accessories such as cables and circuit boards to imply a fascination with technology.

ECO Short for ecology/ecological, Eco has become a generalized prefix that signifies an association with environmental issues, such as 'eco-friendly' or 'eco-warrior'. Eco-aware attitudes, activities and products have become important components in late 20th-century Western counterculture. It is impossible to pinpoint one particular style for Eco but there are certain kinds of clothing which became popular amongst this social group; recycled clothing, patchwork clothes, hemp, reconstructed clothes, handmade and traditional ethnic clothes are all common.

FETISH Describes the attire worn by the growing number of people who choose fetishistic clothing such as rubber, PVC, stiletto heels, thigh-high boots and corsets. In 1983 the first one-nighter fetish club, Skin Two, opened in Soho in London. Aided by designers such as Murray and Vern, fetish clothing is now a major influence on street, mainstream and high fashion.

FUNK Black American dance music of the 1970s. This music was also associated with radical Black politics and the re-awakening of a Black American consciousness. As is often the case, Funk crossed over and quickly began appealing to a white audience, particularly in Britain where pop/rock music was not niche-marketed for specific radical groupings. The style is loud and ostentatious; platform shoes, satin and lamé jumpsuits, huge jewellery and lots of glittery stage make-up contributed to the Funk look.

GAY STYLE Designates the various dress codes associated with the Gay and Lesbian scene which often play on and parody 'accepted' notions of dress, gender and sexuality. Paradoxically, Gay style often filters back into the 'straight' world. British pop music, in particular, has grown adept at using this source when packaging its stars – examples include David Bowie, Take That, Wham!, and even the early Beatles.

GLAM ROCK/GLAM A term with split connotations. It refers to early 1970s glitter-era music and clothes, typified by silver lurex, cork-soled platforms, men in make-up, and personified, for example, by Gary Glitter, David Bowie and The New York Dolls. It is also used to describe a particular brand of 1980s Heavy Metal music that served up a curious mix of bare-chested machismo and androgynous posturing.

GOTH An abbreviation of the word Gothic, it became synonymous with a look that grew out of an early 1980s club scene initially centred around The Batcave in London's Leicester Square. Black clothing (with a hint of purple), often with fetishistic, historical, religious or occult references, deathly pale complexions, black and red cosmetics, heavy silver jewellery and black, spiky hair characterize this style.

GREASERS The name given in the late 1960s to British bikers who had a distinct image. They wore frayed, oil-soaked jeans, Second World War helmets or peaked leather caps and cut-down leather jackets.

GRUNGE First appearing in the late 1980s, Grunge – America's answer to Punk Rock – described both a new generation of loud, guitar-orientated rock music and the attitude of its exponents. In the US, Grunge became associated with the music of groups such as Nirvana and Pearl Jam, as well as providing an identity and soundtrack for the 'lost' Generation X'ers, the (generally) white, middle-class young people who could never hope to maintain, or even want, the same levels of economic and material achievement as their parents.

GRUNGE (UK) In Britain, Grunge was the name given by the music press to a loose and short-lived collective of new rock bands, such as Gaye Bikers on Acid, Rage Against the Machine and Pop Will Eat Itself, who were heralded in about 1987-8 as being the 'next big thing'. The word has since been used to describe the attitude, scruffiness and loud music preferred by youth who identify with this music. Grunge style, or rather anti-style, is a combination of second-hand clothing (jumpers, jackets) worn with faded denim and heavy boots. Other items associated with Grunge are checked lumberjack shirts, well-worn leather jackets and long, tangled hair.

HEAD-BANGER Distinguishes a fan of Heavy Metal/Rock Music. It derives from the violent head-shaking dance that is often practised by 'metal heads'. Head-bangers can be seen in a variety of worn-out tour T-Shirts, a similarly worn-out pair of tight denim jeans, sneakers or boots and a badge-encrusted leather or denim jacket.

HIPPY A member of the counterculture movement of the late 1960s. The term Hippies was used to describe politically and hedonistically motivated young people with a distinctive yet diverse style, that included long hair and ethnic Indian and African clothes accompanied by bare feet or sandals.

HIPSTERS In the USA in the 1940s, musicians such as Thelonious Monk and Dizzy Gillespie were playing a new kind of music – Bebop. Hipsters were enthusiasts of this music, and their particular style of dress, with berets, goatee beards, wide colourful scarves and shades, included elements which can still be seen in the 1990s in such streetstyles as Acid Jazz.

INDIE An abbreviation of the word 'independent' and used to describe music released on non-major record labels. This section of the music industry was born out of the DIY approach to record manufacture adopted by many Punk Rock bands during the late 1970s. The Indie style combines a lot of clothes worn in similar streetstyles such as Grunge. Black or retro flowery dresses worn over leggings or stripy tights, torn, faded jeans, tour T-shirts, oversized jumpers, and Dr Marten boots are all characteristic.

JUNGLE A type of music and dress which evolved from Britain's inner cities in the early 1990s. Drum and bass sequences distinguish this urban musical style which is associated with Moschino jeans, silk shirts and smart trainers.

MADCHESTER A corruption of the word Manchester, it was used to describe the white working-class club, drug and music scene that had developed in the city during the late 1980s. Groups often associated with the 'Madchester' era were the Stone Roses, the Happy Mondays and Inspiral Carpets. Littered with drug references, 'Madchester' brought together 1960s Psychedelia, laddish football-terrace nous and elements of Black American music/street culture. The Madchester look was epitomized by Joe Bloggs designs of the time: huge baggy flared trousers worn with long-sleeved T-shirts (usually with a bold print) and Kicker shoes in a pastel colour.

MOD American influences, primarily soul music and language, were absorbed by this quintessentially British post-war youth culture. The Mods – short for Modernists/Moderns – also drew heavily on contemporary ideas about style and design from the Continent (including, for example, the suit, the scooter and even the name). This ability to orchestrate disparate cultural traditions continues to underpin many aspects of British streetstyles. The most common image of Mods is an immaculate, sharply tailored suit over a white button-down shirt with pointed-toe shoes, although a whole variety of looks is adopted by the Mods including Italian sportswear and the renowned parka.

NEW AGE: SEE TRAVELLERS

NORTHERN SOUL A British 1970s dance and fashion craze centred on particular soul clubs in the industrial North and Midlands. The music was obscure Black-American dance noted for its 'stomping' rhythm, and the clothes were based on flared and updated Mod styles, such as 'Oxford bags' blazers, leather macs and white tennis socks.

OLD SKOOL A term widely used by youth-orientated style magazines in 1993 and 1994 to describe the fashion of wearing old styles of sportswear and training shoes, in particular, Adidas Gazelles, Puma Skate trainers and 1970s style tracksuits.

PREPPY Like Ivy League, this is a reading of American students' dress coding. However, in this instance the look is younger – high school rather than university – and more evocative of the 1950s. Preppy style is a mixture of smart casual skirts and trousers, often worn with good quality knitwear (sometimes a twinset) and the ubiquitous deck shoe.

PSYCHEDELIC Defines young people in the mid-1960s who were involved in the counterculture surrounding the hallucinogenic drug LSD. This term is also used to describe styles of dress, graphics and music created during this period. The style was eclectic and ostentatious. People wore artificial fabrics, such as PVC and fake fur, with huge perspex jewellery. Inspired by the visuals induced by an LSD trip, clothing was very colourful and people often painted their faces and bodies in similar patterns. A lot of clothing came from second-hand shops, creating a retro feel.

PSYCHOBILLY Member of a subgenre of the early 1980s Rockabilly movement. Psychobillies were inspired by the style and sound of the American band, The Cramps. They were identifiable by their quiffs and customized leather and denim clothes.

PUNK A British subculture of the mid-1970s epitomized by the look and attitude of the Sex Pistols. The style most often associated with Punk involves bondage trousers worn with ripped T-shirts with anarchic slogans and boots. Hair and make-up was an integral part of Punk – hair was dyed violently bright colours and made to stand up on end, and facial piercing (particularly cheeks and noses) became popular.

RAGGA The prefix of the word 'Raggamuffin', which was originally a derogatory term for delinquent Jamaican youths. Ragga began in the mid-1980s in Jamaican dancehalls and has since spread worldwide. The lyrics of the music associated with Ragga, performed by musicians such as Shabba Ranks, are aspirational, as is the dress and ostentatious fabrics with elaborate detailing.

RASTA The word 'Rasta', from Rastafarian, comes from 'Ras Tafari', one of the titles of the late Emperor of Ethiopia, Haile Selassie. Rastafarianism merged with the subculture which had grown up around reggae and gave the movement new impetus. It was spread still further by Bob Marley and other reggae musicians throughout the late 1970s and 1980s. A typical Rasta outfit would consist of utilitarian jacket and trousers worn over a T-shirt in the same colours as the Ethiopian flag (red, gold and green), and a tam (knitted cap) over dreadlocks.

RAVE When Acid House music became popular in the UK in the late 1980s, enormous parties were held in warehouses and large venues around the country. Young people, often fuelled by the drug ecstasy, would converge to dance until dawn at these so-called Raves. One of the early looks associated with Acid House is that of Ibizan clubs, with lots of bright layered clothes (some reminiscent of Hippy style) in acid colours and bandannas. T-shirts printed with Smiley faces were very popular.

ROCKABILLY: SEE WORKWEAR ROCKABILLY

ROCKERS Describes British bikers in the 1960s. They were first known as Ton-Up Boys due to their obsession with travelling at 100 mph on their bikes. Their respective styles were slightly different: Rockers wore black leather jackets decorated with metal studs and hand-painted insignia, whilst the Ton-Up Boys' style was much simpler and more functional.

RUDE BOY The Rude Boys of the early 1960s were young Jamaican men who listened to Bluebeat, Ska and Rocksteady music. They had a distinctive dress code of shiny suits and snap-brim hats which was revived in Britain in the 1980s.

SKATER First used in the 1950s in the USA for (mainly) adolescent boys who practised skateboarding. Skaters have always been associated with Surfers in terms of style and attitude. This also applies to Snowboarders because the sport is seen as 'Snow Surfing'.

SKINHEAD Described the working-class youth cult which evolved from the Mod style in 1967. The Skinheads' look consisted of button-down shirts, Levi jeans and loafers worn with a shaved head (crew cut).

SOUL/SOUTHERN SOUL/'SOULIES' Soul Boys and Girls were a mainly working-class subculture in Britain in the mid-1970s, defined by its identification with soul music. Soul Boy style had certain trademark elements such as white socks worn with pumps or Chinese slippers, and a Wedge haircut.

STREETSTYLE/SUBCULTURAL STYLE Describes the dress code associated with a particular subcultural group, which differs from mainstream fashion and denotes a desire to identify with like-minded people.

SURFER Used since the 1950s for someone who takes part in the sport of surfing. It refers to the distinctive dress of Surfers, which has always differed from the mainstream. The early Surfer style incorporated Hawaiian shirts, shorts and quiff haircuts, whereas in the nineties Surfers prefer the baggy style of labels such as Quicksilver, worn with Vans trainers and long messy hair.

TECHNO A form of computer-generated music which originated from Detroit in the late 1980s. When the free festival and Rave scenes merged in the late 1980s, such travelling sound systems as Spiral Tribe and Circus Bedlam were formed to organize parties where this industrial-sounding, frenzied rhythm of around 135 beats per minute was played.

TEDDY BOYS Members of the first recognizable British youth cult. They were initially known as New Edwardians, because of the frock coats and decorative waistcoats they wore with 'stovepipe' (later 'drainpipe') trousers.

TRAVELLER Came into use in Britain during the 1980s to describe people who had chosen to live an alternative lifestyle on the road. They are often labelled New Age due to the spiritual beliefs some of them share. It is difficult to pinpoint a single style to travellers but they often wear many layers of second-hand clothing, a pair of Para boots (army boots) and have dreadlocked hair often dyed, wrapped and beaded.

TWO TONE A youth cult in Britain during the late 1970s and early 1980s. It is associated with bands such as Madness and The Beat. The dress style of Two Tone was a mixture of Mod and Skinhead clothes such as tonik suits, button-down shirts, pork-pie hats and parkas.

WORKWEAR ROCKABILLY A style which became popular amongst British youth at the end of the 1970s. The look was an exaggeration of the 1950s 'hillbilly' Country and Western style. Rockabilly also described a concurrent style epitomized by Elvis in 1956. This look was much smarter: immaculate suits and white shorts instead of frayed denim and workwear.

YARDIES Jamaican men in the 1960s who were often involved in organized crime and had a particular style of smart, aspirational dress.

YOUNG BRITISH RADICAL A particular subcultural style of the 1950s applied predominantly to left-wing British students, and associated with Socialist politics, utilitarian dress and protest music.

ZOOT SUITER A man who wore Zoot Suits, usually Black or Chicano Americans at the end of the 1930s. The term became more widespread through the 1940s among jazz musicians. The Zoot Suit was a highly exaggerated outfit which evolved from the traditional 1930s male two-piece. A long single-breasted drape jacket with extra wide shoulders, wide lapels and multibuttoned wrists was worn over loose, high-waisted, pleated trousers which tapered to very narrow pegs at the ankle. The look was finished off with wide-brimmed hats, and a watch on a chain worn hanging from the jacket.

COW BOY & WESTERN

USA ★ LATE 1940S

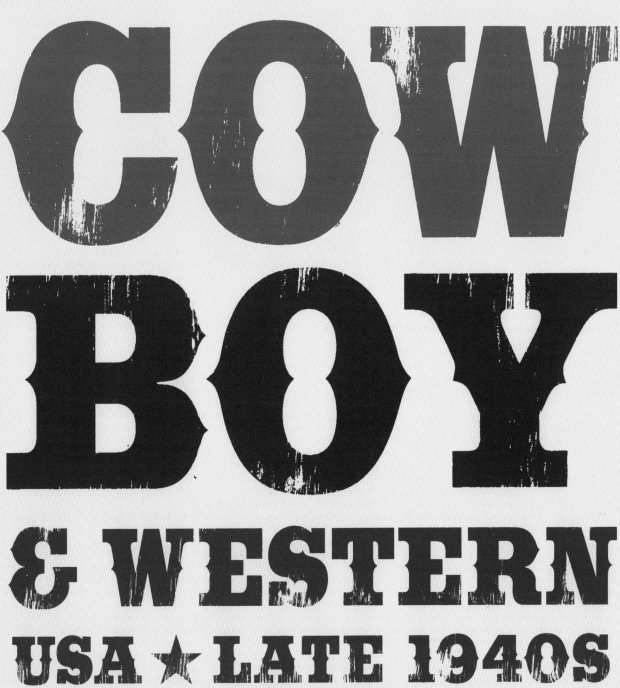

(MAIN) ★ GREEN AND SAND EMBROIDERED AND PIPED WOOL SHIRT, BEN THE RODEO TAILOR ★ PRINTED RAYON 'ROY ROGERS' BANDANNA ★ FELT HAT, ROCKMOUNT RANCHWEAR ★ WORSTED TWILL TROUSERS, SMITH & CHANDLER INDIAN TRADERS ★ PAINTED AND EMBOSSED MODERN LEATHER BELT ★ LEATHER BOOTS WITH CUTWORK

COWBOY AND WESTERN CLOTHES ARE PRACTICAL, DURABLE AND DECORATIVE ★ THE SHIRT HAS A STRONG DOUBLE THICKNESS YOKE AND HALF-MOON POCKETS, REINFORCED WITH STITCHED ARROW HEADS ★ SNAP FASTENINGS PERMIT CLOTHES TO OPEN QUICKLY IF CAUGHT ON A HORN OR A BRANCH ★ THE EMBROIDERED TEXAN ROSE DESIGN SEEN ON THE SHIRT, IS A POPULAR COWBOY STYLE MOTIF WHICH EMBLAZONS MANY GARMENTS ★ A BANDANNA ADDS A TOUCH OF COLOUR AND CAN BE PULLED OVER THE FACE FOR PROTECTION

★ COMPILED BY CHERRY PARKER ★ 'ROY ROGERS' BANDANNA LENT BY KATRINA BEATTY ★

(TOP) ★ COWBOY & WSTERN REVIVAL ★ USA 1990S ★ GREIGE TWO-PIECE POLYESTER SUIT, H-BAR-C CALIFORNIA RANCH WEAR ★ POLY-COTTON SHIRT, H-BAR-C ★ COLLAR STUDS ★ CLIP-ON MAVERICK TIE ★ FELT STETSON-STYLE HAT ★ HOG-SKIN BOOTS, LA GRAN BOTA, MEXICO, LATE 1940S WITH REPLICA TOE-CAPS

WESTERN STYLE SUITS HAVE BEEN WORN FOR EVENING WEAR FROM AROUND 1910 AND THIS TWO-PIECE WAS MADE TO AN ORIGINAL LATE 1940S/EARLY 1950S PATTERN ★ IT RETAINS THE PRACTICAL FEATURES OF CLOTHES WORN IN THE SADDLE, INCLUDING FLAP POCKETS TO SECURE CONTENTS AND QUICK RELEASE SNAP FASTENINGS ★ SOME ELEMENTS, SUCH AS ARROW MOTIFS, BASED ON THE STITCHED ARROW HEADS USED TO REINFORCE POCKET EDGING, BECAME PURELY DECORATIVE ★ H-BAR-C RANCH WEAR BY HALPERN & CHRISTENFELD IS BASED IN NEW YORK AND SUPPLIES THE URBAN COWBOY

★ COMPILED BY CHERRY PARKER ★

(BOTTOM) ★ FASHION COWGIRL ★ GIANNI VERSACE ★ ITALY SPRING/SUMMER 1992 ★ BLACK FRINGED AND STUDDED LEATHER WAISTCOAT AND TROUSERS, PRINTED SILK FOULARD BLOUSE WITH BEADED FRINGING, LEATHER BOOTS

'NOTHING IN THIS WORLD IS MORE AMERICAN THAN A WILD WESTERN LOOK ★ THE GREAT WILD WEST REVIVAL THAT WE ARE EXPERIENCING PROBABLY DEPENDS ON AMERICA'S NEED TO TAKE POSSESSION OF ITS ROOTS AGAIN, WHILE EUROPE FEELS A GREAT ATTRACTION TOWARDS THE REFRESHING WESTERN MYTHS - AND TOWARDS A LOOK THAT SPEAKS OF WIDE-OPEN SPACES AND OF TRADITIONAL WAYS' (VERSACE QUOTED IN VOGUE, MAY 1992, P.131)

★ GIVEN BY GIANNI VERSACE ★

ZOOT SUITER USA (1994 REPLICA)

Black & white chalk-striped wool two-piece suit, printed rayon scarf, Cherry Parker; original 1940s hat

Helen Rose's costume designs for the film *'Stormy Weather'* are among the few surviving sources showing female zoot suits. The two-piece worn by Lena Horne in a dance routine formed the basis for this reproduction, which captures the exaggerated 1940s styling favoured by female Zoot suiters.

Hat lent by Philomena Papirnik. Compiled by Cherry Parker

1943

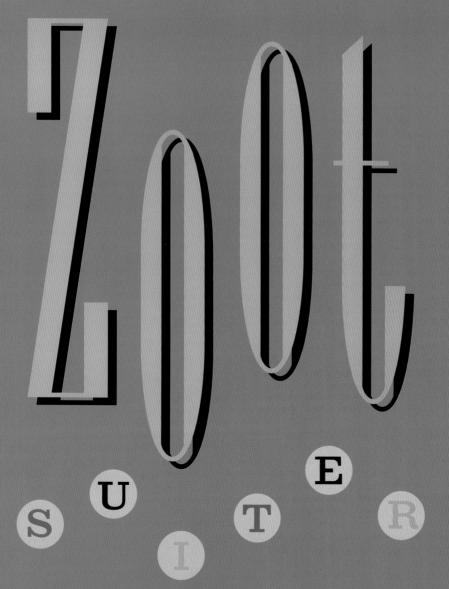

Zoot
SUITER

ZOOT SUITER USA (1994 REPLICA)

Pale green wool two-piece suit, cotton shirt, wool bow-tie, Chris Ruocco Tailors; satin handkerchief, leather and elastic, braces; leather shoes, 1940s

This outfit reveals the extremely long jacket and high cut, baggy, trousers favoured by Zoot Suiters in early 1940s America. Unable to find an original zoot suit, this replica was commissioned. It was based upon the colourful and flamboyant suits worn by Cab Calloway in the 1943 film *'Stormy Weather'*. The zoot suit was revived in the early 1980s by musicians such as Chris Sullivan's band Blue Rondo à la Turk and Kid Creole.

Compiled by Chris Sullivan

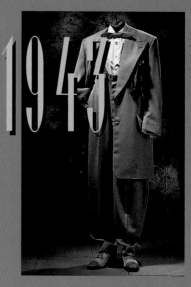

1943

FASHION ZOOT SUIT BETTY JACKSON UK AUTUMN-WINTER 1982 (RE-MADE 1994)

Black crêpe trouser suit with braces, wool shirt with print by Brian Bolger of 'The Cloth', wool crêpe tie, leather shoes: Pied a Terre

'Why a zoot suit? I have always been inspired by "cross dressing" and the idea that women usually look better than men in men's clothes. Hence, the idea of a man's suit always hovers somewhere in the background of a collection. We took just one of these influences and made it our own.' (Betty Jackson)

Given by Betty Jackson

1982

USA LATE 1940S/EARLY 1950S (1994 REPLICA) BLUE DOUBLE-BREASTED WOOL SUIT, SATIN CRAVAT, COTTON SHIRT, SATIN POCKET HANDKERCHIEF, CHRIS RUOCCO TAILORS; LEATHER SHOES, RUPERT; BRACES

hipster

THIS OUTFIT RECREATES THE STYLE OF BEBOP/COOL CAT JAZZ MUSICIANS, SUCH AS DIZZY GILLESPIE AND THELONIOUS MONK, WHICH WAS PICKED UP BY THEIR WHITE AS WELL AS BLACK FANS. IT WAS A DISTINCTIVE LOOK COMBINING THE FASHIONABLE, ROOMY, DOUBLE-BREASTED SUIT WITH DISTINCTIVE ACCESSORIES. COMPILED BY CHRIS SULILIVAN

HIPSTER USA 1980S RED FELT BERET THE MUSIC OF HIPSTER MUSICIAN SLIM GAILLARD - THE MAN WHOSE TROUSERS WERE SAID TO BE 'SHARPER THAN A GILETTE BLADE' IN THE 1940S - ENJOYED A REVIVAL IN THE LATE 1970S. HE REMAINED TRUE TO HIS ORIGINAL STYLE BUT ADDED A BERET (ALWAYS RED OR WHITE) WHICH HE CUSTOMIZED BY WASHING AND STRETCHING IT, SOMETIMES PULLING OFF THE TAIL AND WEARING THE BRIM ON THE OUTSIDE.

WHEN PERFORMING, HE WORE IT TILTED AT A JAUNTY ANGLE AND PULLED IT DEEP DOWN OVER HIS BROW WHEN HE WAS IN THE STREET. IT WAS SAID THAT YOU COULD TELL SLIM'S MOOD BY THE WAY HE WORE HIS BERET. WORN BY SLIM GAILLARD. ANONYMOUS GIFT

BEAT- Leather jacket with
sheepskin lining,
Steerhide; cotton plaid
shirt; cotton T-shirt;
cotton trousers, Tennessee
Overall Company;
leather ex-army boots

This outfit simulates one of
the looks favoured by the
original Beats in the XXXX
circle. Perceived as being
Neil Cassady and Jack Kerouac
almost 'sloppy', it was a pow-
erful anti-establishment and
anti-grey-flannel-suit
statement. It pre-dates the
Beatniks, XXXX XXXXXXXX who
married French existentialist
leanings towards black, with
various Beat elements.

Compiled with advice from
Adrien Henri

USA 1950S

BEATNIK USA/UK late 1950s

Black nylon leotard;
cotton jersey skirt, 1990s;
leather ballet shoes

'The Beatniks came after the forties
when everything was Doris Day ᴀᴀ
and this was the complete opposite.
The hair was the most noticeable
thing - it was always very long.
A lot of the girls were interested
in dance so they would wear leo-
tards and ballet shoes, there were
always lots of these in charity
stores so they could buy them
cheaply. Some of them wore woolly
scarves... they were all covered up
from head to tow in black - like a
bunch of crows!' (Carolyn Cassady).

Compiled by Carolyn Cassady
Skirt given by Carolyn Cassady

B E A T N I K :

FASHION BEATNIK YVES SAINT LAURENT
HAUTE COUTURE, FRANCE,
AUTUMN/WINTER 1963-4

Black ciré peaked balaclava, ciré
jacket, studded suede tunic, cotton
tights, patent-leather thigh-high
boots, kid gloves

Yves Saint Laurent was possibly the
first high fashion designer to
derive inspiration from subcultural
styles. When he was head designer at
Dior, he incorporated all-black
Rocker and Left Bank existentialist
looks into his collections. He opened
his own House in 1962 and has
continued to use these sources as
inspiration. Yves Saint Laurent
selected this outfit from his pri-
vate museum in Paris, to reveal the
Beatnik ɪɴꜰᴜᴇɴᴄᴇ influence on his work.

Lent by Yves Saint Laurent

CARIBBEAN STYLE
UK EARLY 1950S
BLACK-AND-WHITE CHECKED
WOOLLEN COAT, KRIMATEX, LONDON;
SCRIM AND VELVET HAT; PLASTIC MOCK-CROC BAG;
COTTON MIX TWO-PIECE SUIT, NAT GAYNES, GUYANA

Dr Gilroy came to England from Guyana in 1952. Her wardrobe consisted of brightly coloured clothes, which she had made by local dressmakers, copying styles from American fashion magazines. She wore this pink suit in the Caribbean and bought the hat and coat in London because of the colder climate. She states that her clothes were significantly more colourful than standard post-war British wear and included items such as peddle-pushers, which had not previously been seen in Britain. Worn and given by Dr Beryl Gilroy

CARIBBEAN STYLE
UK MID-1950S
BLACK FELT HAT; POLY-WOOL SUIT
WITH HORN BUTTONS, D.A. LILLIARD;
COTTON SHIRT; SILK TIE; LEATHER SHOES

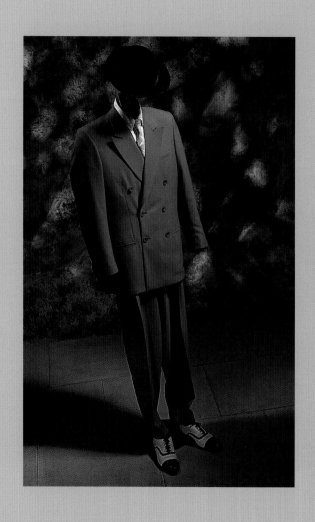

This outfit was recreated by Derek Lilliard who was advised by Caribbean fabric suppliers, the tailor Mark Savile and members of his own family, who came to Britain in the 1950s. In the Caribbean it was common for men to wear such brightly coloured, generously cut suits on an everyday basis, and they continued to do so when they emigrated. In addition to their flamboyant use of colour the cut of suits made in the Caribbean was distinctive: trousers were high waisted, had low seats and baggy legs which tapered to a 16-inch hem with a 2-inch turn-up. They were teamed with double-breasted jackets with wide lapels. These 'sharp' suits provided a lively contrast to the more conservative cut and colours favoured by other British men. Compiled by Derek Lilliard

SURFER USA 1950s

BLUE PRINTED COTTON HAWAIIAN SHIRT; DUPONT'S SUPPLEX SURF TRUNKS, PATAGONIA, USA, 1990s BASED ON 1950s ORIGINALS

The printed cotton Hawaiian shirt with wood buttons is an original. The trunks, made in quick-drying Supplex, are based on a 1950s cotton design, retaining the triple stitched seams for strength and inner pocket for valuables. Surf shorts have become larger and were often worn by 1980s Skaters and B-Boys, while Hawaiian shirts were worn by Rockabillies and Soul Boys/Girls in the 1970s.

SURFER UK 1993
WHITE AND BLACK COTTON T-SHIRT WITH PUFF INK SCREEN-PRINTED DESIGN, BUZ; COTTON CHECK SHORTS, STUSSY, USA; BRUSHED COTTON PLAID SHIRT, COUNTRY, USA; RUBBER AND NYLON SANDALS, REEF, BRAZIL; RUBBER AND CANVAS BASKETBALL SHOES, CONVERSE

This surf outfit encompasses items which have stylistic links with a number of subcultures. The 'World Tribe' Stussy shorts, designed by Surfer and Skateboarder Shaun Stussy, have been adopted by B-Boys. Conversely, Buz's 'surfwear and streetfashion' T-shirt was inspired by mid-1980s baggy Rave clothing. These styles have also been appropriated by many other subcultures. Only the labels distinguish them as surfwear. T-shirt given by Jasper Humphris, Buz. Shorts given by Gimme 5/Stussy. Shirt given by Shaun Turpin. Converse given by Ollie Fitzgerald

FASHION SURFER
KARL LAGERFELD FOR CHANEL FRANCE SPRING/SUMMER 1991 YELLOW SEQUINNED SILK AND GROSGRAIN JACKET, COTTON AND LYCRA LEGGINGS; SANDALS, REEF

This long-line jacket was inspired by the construction of Neoprene wetsuits and was made with wetlook sea blue and sunshine yellow sequins. Outfits were modelled on the Paris catwalk by Christy Turlington and Linda Evangelista, who carried surf boards as accessories. Given by the House of Chanel

gay style uk 1988

purple stretch satin hat and bodysuit,
James Montgomery; corduroy jacket,
Leigh Bowery; leather Dr Martens boots

At this time, Cornelius Brady revelled
in wearing flamboyant and outré
clothes. Club host and performance
artist Leigh Bowery made the jacket
for Brady. 'People were completely
shocked when I wore it to Tesco's
and it looked good with a big trolley!'
Bowery had previously worked with
fashion company Bodymap and
continued to make clothes for friends.
James Montgomery (pattern cutter for
Richmond Cornejo) created this unique
body suit and hat.

worn and given by Cornelius Brady

gay & lesbian

lesbian style uk 1971

orange feather boa and purple cotton
jersey dress, Biba, 1971; crochet wool
waistcoat made by wearer

'I wore this Biba dress to the first Gay
Liberation Front Ball, which was held
at the old Kensington Town Hall.
I wore long purple boots from Anello
and Davide with it. This was the period
of positive (i.e. not sexless) hippie
androgyny, and butch was definitely
not politically correct. Quite a few
lesbians wore Biba clothes, and they
were even more commonly worn by
feminists generally. I gave my other
full length Biba dress (a cream satin,
Jean Harlow number) to a gay man for
drag. I always loved Biba and have never
ceased to miss it' (Elizabeth Wilson).

worn and given by Elizabeth Wilson

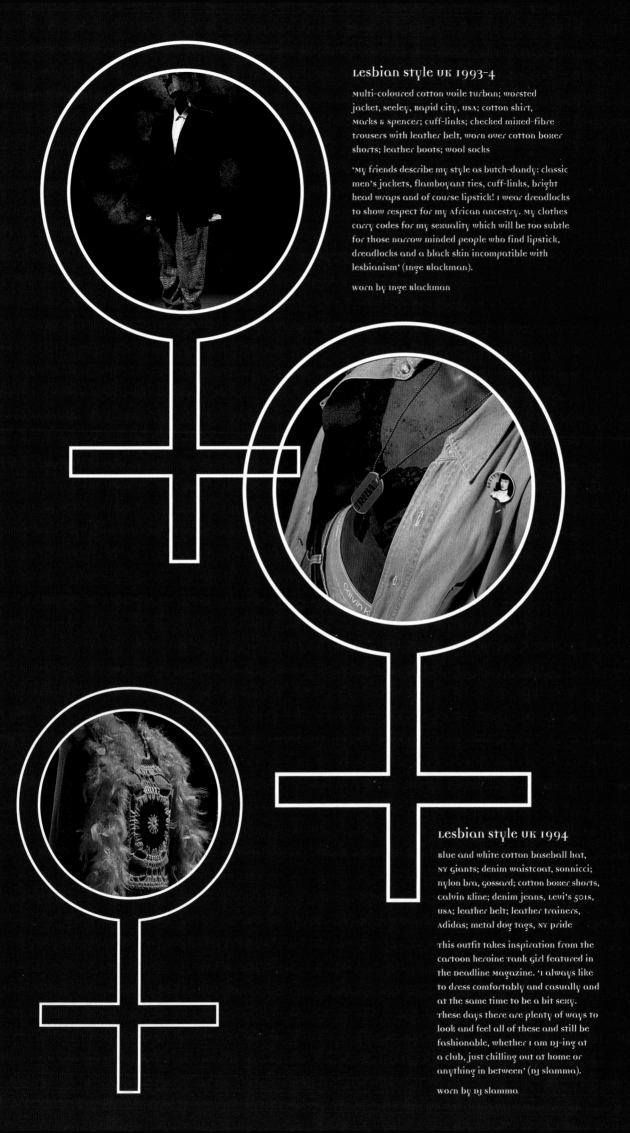

lesbian style uk 1993-4

multi-coloured cotton voile turban; worsted jacket, seeley, rapid city, usa; cotton shirt, marks & spencer; cuff-links; checked mixed-fibre trousers with leather belt, worn over cotton boxer shorts; leather boots; wool socks

'my friends describe my style as butch-dandy: classic men's jackets, flamboyant ties, cuff-links, bright head wraps and of course lipstick! i wear dreadlocks to show respect for my african ancestry. my clothes carry codes for my sexuality which will be too subtle for those narrow minded people who find lipstick, dreadlocks and a black skin incompatible with lesbianism' (inge blackman).

worn by inge blackman

lesbian style uk 1994

blue and white cotton baseball hat, ny giants; denim waistcoat, sonnicci; nylon bra, gossard; cotton boxer shorts, calvin kline; denim jeans, levi's 501s, usa; leather belt; leather trainers, adidas; metal dog tags, ny pride

this outfit takes inspiration from the cartoon heroine tank girl featured in the deadline magazine. 'i always like to dress comfortably and casually and at the same time to be a bit sexy. these days there are plenty of ways to look and feel all of these and still be fashionable, whether i am dj-ing at a club, just chilling out at home or anything in between' (dj slamma).

worn by dj slamma

gay style uk

early to mid-1990s checked cotton shirt,
Anvil, 1994; leather-fronted waistcoat,
Madhouse, 1994; denim jeans, Levi's 501s,
USA, 1993; leather belt, 1990; wool
walking socks; leather shoes, Dolcis, 1993

Justin Stubbings has worn this style of
dress for the last 15 years, and it is a
look he intends to retain - 'it is rooting'.
He acknowledges and likes the influence
of western styling. Levi's are worn for
their cut and fit: he rubs them with a
pumice stone to emphasize the contours
of the body. The look is updated with
the leather waistcoat, which was
traditionally associated with the fetish
scene, but has moved into the mainstream.
This style of dress is currently enjoying
popularity among lesbians.

worn by Justin Stubbings

gay

gay style uk 1994

black ma1 jacket; cotton vest; woollen
kilt; woollen hiking socks; logger
boots, georgia, usa; leather belt;
necklace with freedom rings

'the flight jacket, vest and boots are
staple gay garments often seen as
cliché clone wear. the kilt added a new
dimension when it was first worn
publicly by the gay community in 1993
at the new york pride march. this outfit
is an exact copy of one my friend ray
wore in 1994 in london' (shaun cole).

outfit compiled by shaun cole
boots given by office shoes

gay style uk mid-1950s

printed cotton bolero shirt; striped
cotton jeans, vince; canvas deck
shoes, 1990s

vince was opened on newbergh street,
london, in 1954 by bill green and, as
john gielgud states, catered for
'chelsea homosexuals, artists and
theatricals, muscle boys' (nik cohn,
today there are no gentlemen).
john hardy worked in the shop and
modelled for the mail-order catalogue
before he became a highly successful
full-time model. the shop's merchandise
was distinctive because it was ahead
of its time and was influenced by
continental european styling.

worn and given by john hardy

Preppy USA

PREPPY STYLE was casual, sporty, wholesome and clean cut. Blazers, with natural shoulders, three buttons and straight cut pocket flaps were worn with untapered shirts with button-down collars. Trousers were always cut straight with narrow turn-ups.

Compiled and given by JOHN SIMON

PREPPY USA 1950s
Navy-blue wool blazer; cotton shirt;
Tie; Acrilan trousers;
leather penny loafer shoes

THE DISTINCTIVE PREPPY collegiate blazer and button-down shirt is worn by both sexes, but women's garments are often in bright or pastel colours, such as the pink shirt seen here. Preppy women announced their femininity by the traditional, well-tried formula of round-necked cardigan and full skirt. The emphasis is upon fine-quality clothes, classic styling and meticulous colour co-ordination. Stick-pins became fashionable Preppy accessories during the late 1970s and early 1980s.

Stickpin on loan
Compiled by KATRINA BEATTY

EARLY 1980s

Navy wool blazer; Oxford cloth shirt; wool jumper with floral yoke patterning;

cotton twill skirt; gold metal stick pin with heart motif;

wool tights; leather penny loafer shoes, complete with American penny inserts

YOUNG BRITISH RADICAL

UK 1958-63

CAMEL-COLOURED WOOL DUFFLE
COAT WITH <u>CND</u> BADGE :
WOOL SCARF TO MATCH
CND COLOURS, 1990's;
WOOL EX-NAVAL SWEATER
WOOL SKIRT; WOOL STOCKINGS
LEATHER LACE-UP SHOES

'THE CLOTHES WERE ABSOLUTELY NOT AN END IN
THEMSELVES — NOONE DISCUSSED THEM OR
SEEMINGLY TOOK AN INTEREST IN THEM.
WE WORE PRACTICAL CHEAP AND COMFORTABLE
CLOTHES FOR ACTIVE CAMPAIGNING.

WE WORE VERY LITTLE MAKE-UP AND ESCHEWED
CONVENTIONAL NOTIONS OF YOUNG WOMEN
IN THE 1950s, THROUGH APPROPRIATION OF
LOOSE AND COMFORTABLE MEN'S CLOTHING.

IT NEEDS TO BE REMEMBERED THAT IT DID NOT
TAKE MUCH THEN, EITHER IN DRESS OR POLITICAL
TERMS TO CAUSE A PUBLIC SHOCK (LOU TAYLOR)

COMPILED BY LOU TAYLOR

'I AM LOOKING FOR LASTING DURABILITY
IN MY CLOTHES. I WOULD LIKE THEM TO
LAST AS FURNITURE OR OBJECTS DO.
FOR THAT REASON MY PREFERRED MATERIALS
ARE THOSE WHICH ARE THE MOST RESISTANT
OVER TIME'...
(JEAN-CHARLES DE CASTELBAJAC).

FASHION RADICAL

JEAN-CHARLES DE CASTELBAJAC
FRANCE AUTUMN/WINTER 1990-1
GREY WOOL DUFFLE COAT WITH
LEATHER TRIM
GIVEN BY JEAN-CHARLES DE CASTELBAJAC

TEDDY BOY

rEVIVAL

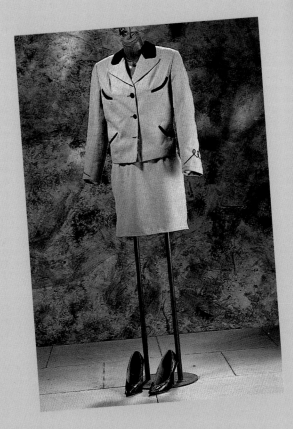

NEW EDWARDIAN
UK EARLY 1950s

Pinstriped charcoal wool three-piece suit, Denaman and Goddard, Eton; striped cotton shirt, Harvey and Hudson, St James's; collar, Mastocroft; printed rayon tie, Tootal; bowler, Dunn & Co; leather Oxford brogues, 1970s

'There is a new almost Edwardian formality in men's London clothes, which is reminiscent of the pre-1914 period.' (Vogue, April 1950)

It was this elite look that became the stylistic catalyst for Teddy Boys. The suit was originally made for Squadron Leader Bayley, and the collar belonged to Ian Grant Esq., a well-known New Edwardian.

Worn (1979) and lent by Stephen Calloway

TEDDY GIRL REVIVAL
UK 1970s

Wool jacket with cotton velvet trim; metal necklace with rose pendant; wool skirt; leather stiletto shoes, 1960s

The tailored suit, with Western-style pockets, was originally made-to-measure for Angelene Webb in 1970. It was subsequently given to her niece, who wore it during the late 1970s. She re-made the skirt, which had worn out from continuous wear. This style of dress was typical among Teddy Girls throughout the 1970s - the jacket has retained the early tailored style, but the skirt is short, in line with 1970s mainstream fashion. Very high-heeled stiletto and pointed court shoes from the 1960s were worn for day and evening.

Worn by Angelene and Lou Webb and lent by Lou Webb

TEDDY BOY REVIVAL UK 1964

(above) Grey jacket, wool and terelene with silk velvet trim, Alexandre, 1964

This jacket forms part of Dave Forrest's first Teddy Boy suit, which he had made-to-measure from Alexandre, a tailor working in North Shields, Tyne and Wear. He specified the particular detailing he wanted, such as the velvet trim on the cuffs and the half belt, also in black velvet, on the back. When he purchased this suit, Dave Forrest was aged 17 years and was working as an apprentice. The suit cost £16, which represented four weeks wages. The trousers were subsequently worn out. (The V&A also has jackets from the Teddy Boy suits worn by Dave Forrest in 1965 and 1966.)

Worn by Dave Forrest

FASHION TED LEE BENDER UK 1976

(re-made 1994)
(below) Red and black cotton velvet trouser suit

'The Teds have rocked back the fashion clock ... It's the clothes of the fifties that are really going top of the pops. Drape jackets, velvet collars, DA haircuts, luminous socks and beetle crushers is the gear that's go'.

(Lesley Ebbetts reviewing Lee Bender's Teddy Boy revival collection, *Daily Mirror*, 23 September 1976)

TEDDY GIRL REVIVAL UK 1954

(left) Black barathea and silk velvet, Weaver to Wearer, 1954

'I felt the bees-knees in this jacket. I saved for it and really loved it and that's why I kept it for 40 years. It still fits me and I still love it!' (Pat Essam).

The Northampton-based tailor Weaver to Wearer made this jacket for Patricia Essam in 1954, when she was aged 16 years. It cost approximately £10. She wore it with red tartan trousers and leather sandals, which laced up the leg, or with a black skirt and winkle-picker stiletto-heeled shoes.

Worn by Patricia Essam (née Goodman)

TEDDY BOY
UK c1970

REVIVAL

Grey and black worsted and velvet three-piece suit, Hardy Amies for Hepworth; nylon shirt, Burlington; bootlace tie; leather shoes

Hardy Amies commented that 'Teddy Boys were showing a sort of pantomime version of Edwardianism' (*Still Here*, 1984). He designed this up-market suit for the elegant Ted, under licence for the Hepworth chain of menswear stores. By 1970 the jackets had more velvet trim (originally it was confined to the collar and cuffs) but retained the classic seamless back. The long drape jacket with drainpipe trousers takes elements from New Edwardian and Zoot Suits and the bootlace tie is a crossover from Western styling.

Compiled by Judy Westacott
Shoes lent by Judy Westacott

ROCKABILLY: UK early 1980s

Black and pink wool jacket, Lambliner, USA, 1950s;
Cotton shirt; wool trousers, 'Rockacha';
Leather shoes, Denson

By the early 1980s many Rockabillies
had adopted a smart, rather flamboyant style,
which drew on 1950s American casual wear.
Original garments such as this jacket
became highly desirable.
The cut of these trousers was based on
those worn by rock star Eddy Cochrane.
'Rockacha', specializing in 1950s-style clothes,
was opened in Kensington Market in 1979
by Jay Strongman and Bob Crossley and rapidly
gained cult status.

Worn by Jay Strongman

Rockabilly

ROCKABILLY UK early 1980s

White cotton knit blouse over satin bra, 1950s;
Cotton check pedal-pushers;
Canvas shoes, 'Sunshines by Bata'

Female Rockabillies went to great lengths
to achieve an authentic 1950s American
teenage appearance by scouring specialist
second-hand shops. This look captured
the naivety and the optimism of young,
post-war America. Quiffed and ponytail
hairstyles and heavy make-up made
the look distinctively Rockabilly.

Compiled by Jay Strongman

ROCKABILLY UK 1979-84

Red rayon shirt with felt decoration,
American, 1950s;
Denim jeans, 'In the style of James Dean'
by J.S.B., USA, 1950s;
Leather loafer shoes, 1980s

Authentic American casual wear
from the 1950s was highly desirable
among Rockabillies of both sexes,
and specialist shops such as
American Classics catered for this demand.
Bowling shirts and original 1950s jeans
were particularly popular for men.
'Alex Nauguchi - General Contractor'
is emblazoned across the back of the shirt.

Compiled by Jay Strongman

ROCKABILLY UK 1977-8

Navy wool & vinyl
donkey jacket; cotton plaid
shirt, USA; bootlace tie;
ripped denim jeans, Lee
Riders; Derby steel
toe-capped boots

These clothes present a
consciously dishevelled look
which was borrowed from
utilitarian working dress.
This unkempt style was
often adopted in reaction to
the overtly smart Teddy Boy
suit of the previous generation.
However, some features
of Teddy Boy dress were
retained, including the
bootlace tie.

Compiled by
Jay Strongman & Judy Westacott

FASHION WORKWEAR/ROCKABILLY
Calvin Klein USA Spring/Summer 1994

Blue denim sleeveless top, jacket, shorts & jeans,
knickers & bra top, leather mules

'I'm inspired by what is American... and jeans
are very American. I'm also inspired by the kids
on the streets and what they are doing...
How they wear their clothes and interpret them...
They have this incredible energy and attitude
that is modern and unpretentious...
They're really into individuality and that's exciting'
(Calvin Klein).

Given by Calvin Klein

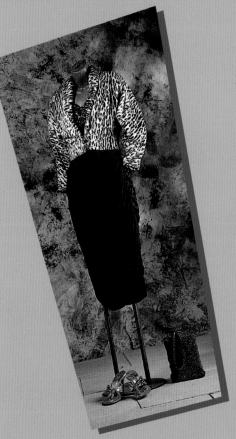

ROCKABILLY/ROCKING SCENE UK 1990

Fake leopard fur jacket, Julian Beller,
California, 1950s; ruched nylon dress,
Pulmarks model, early 1950s; beaded evening
bag; gold leather and fake fur mules, Paul Allen
for Amano, California; costume jewellery

The stylistic focus in the Rocking Scene is
upon genuine 1950s clothes. In the early 1980s,
casual wear was all important but today the look is
overtly glamorous. This outfit was reserved for special
nights out - such as those worn at Hemsby
Rock 'n' Roll weekends. It is enjoyed for its
body-consciousness and femininity and offers
a form of escapism. 'Dressing-up makes
me feel like a different person' (Terrie Ford).

Worn and lent by Terrie Ford

Rockabilly

WORKWEAR/ROCKABILLY
USA/UK 1950s-today

Blue denim jacket, LEVI's 501s, Type 2, USA;
collarless cotton shirt; denim jeans, LEVI's 501s, BXX;
Leather boots, Georgia, USA

LEVI's hard wearing, practical and cheap
clothes were originally worn by miners and
working cowboys. The yellow stitching, visible
selvedge, cuff rivets and 'bar tacking' on the front
reveal the vintage of this jacket, which
was originally worn as a shirt. To facilitate
ease in the saddle these jeans were made
with a twisted seam, rivets on the back
pockets and straight cut legs, so that they
covered the cowboy's boots. Denim workwear
has subsequently been adopted by many
subcultures, but it is among Rockabillies that
these early authentic items are particularly desirable.

Jacket and trousers lent by Peter Rogers
Boots given by Caven Cooper, American Classics

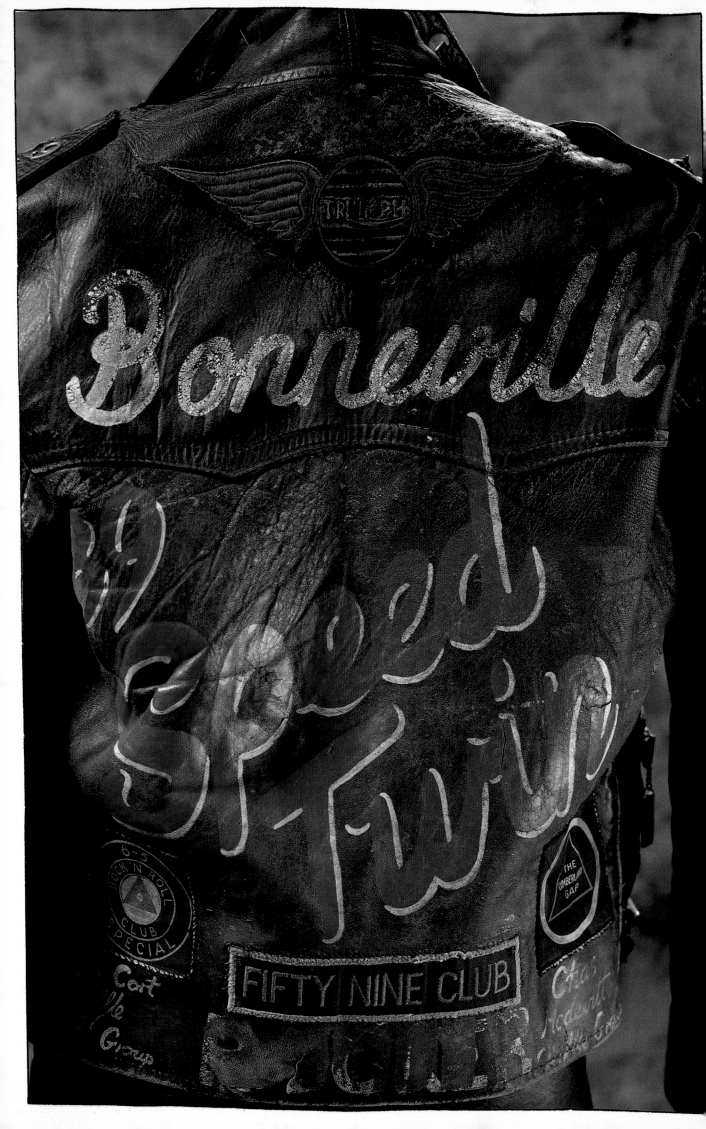

ROCKER

UK MID-1960S

BLACK LEATHER JACKET CUSTOMIZED WITH PAINTED DECORATION AND WITH FABRIC PATCH SHOWING MEMBERSHIP OF THE SPECIALIST ROCKERS CLUB, **The 59 Club**.

Lent by **John Stuart**

ROCKER™

UK 1968

White vinyl and black plastic 'MOBY CAP' crash helmet, CHAS OWEN & Co.(Bow) Ltd

Owen made this helmet to resemble the cap worn by **Marlon Brando** in 1954 cult film **The Wild One**. It was made after the film had been released in Britain, following many years under a censorship ban. It is branded with the British standard Kite mark.

Worn and lent by Nigel Stark

GREASER
UK 1970s

Customized black leather cut-down jacket, with metal studs and BSA patch

LENT BY JOHN STUART

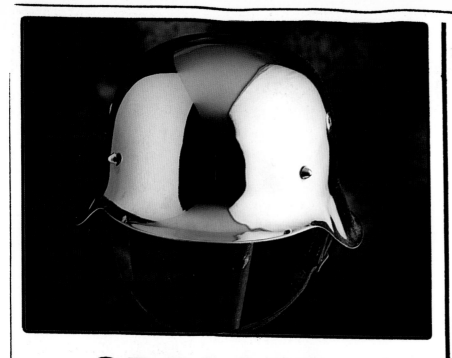

UK **GREASER** 1967-9

Polished
German
tin helmet

Lent by The Tortoise Motorcycle Club

USA
1965 - 9
customized
leather
jacket,
Perfecto

GREASER
UK 1967-9

White cotton T-shirt; customized denim cut-down jacket, LEVI'S, USA; vinyl jeans, IRONGUARD; denim jeans, LEVI'S, USA; leather steel toe-capped boots

Greasers were split into the hardcore **Hells Angels** and mainstream Greasers - these clothes represent the latter's gear. This group was inspired by **American bikers**, who appropriated tin helmets, garments extensively embellished with regalia and cut-downs - jackets with the sleeves cut off. **Greasers'** clothes were scruffier and dirtier than their **Rocker** predecessors. Trousers were often so torn and patched that two pairs were worn together.

Compiled and lent by **John Stuart**

TON-UP BOY

UK early 1960s Vinyl jacket

Jackets worn by **Ton-Up boys** were unadorned. Heavy-duty vinyl was less expensive than leather, but was as durable and was also considered **authentic**.

Lent by John Stuart

ROCKER

TON-UP BOY UK 1956-63

Grey **EVEROAK RACEMASTER JET** helmet with **HALCYON** goggles; silky scarf; knitted rayon scarf; cotton shirt; vinyl jacket, **BELSTAFF**; leather gloves; denim jeans with studded leather belt, **LEVI'S**, USA; sheepskin-lined leather flying boots

It was the bike and its capacity for speed, rather than clothes, that preoccupied **Ton-Up boys** in the 1950s. They wore heavy-duty, practical and largely unadorned clothing. Originally they bought readily available ex-WD (surplus War Department) garments which were low cost.

Compiled and lent by John Stuart

UK 1964-7

Black leather peaked cap with TRIUMPH patch, chains and studs; leather jacket, LEWIS LEATHER, customized with badges, patches, painted slogans; cotton shirt; leather jeans with metal studded leather belt; zipped leather commando-style boots

Moving on from the essentially plain look of the **Ton-Up boy**, by the mid-1960s **Rockers** emerged, with a fully fledged style of their own. They were distinctly recognizable with their customized clothing, emblazoned with painted slogans, patches and studding. This outfit's jacket has a fabric **59 Club** patch across the back. This style was also adopted by '**bus-stop**' Rockers.

Compiled and lent by John Stuart

FASHION ROCKER

KATHARINE HAMNETT UK AUTUMN/WINTER 1989-90

BLACK LEATHER JACKET WITH METAL STUDS

Katharine Hamnett brought peace and ecological issues to the forefront in 1983 with her **'Choose Life'** collection, and subsequently garments with inscriptions became one of her signatures. Of **'Clean Up or Die'** she states **'We were trying to make an environmental message sexy'** (Katharine Hamnett).

Given by Katharine Hamnett

FASHION ROCKER

JOHN RICHMOND *UK Spring/Summer 1988*

Printed black leather jacket

'The inspiration was to take two very strong reference points - the leather jacket and tattoos - that signify youth and rebellion' (John Richmond).

Given by John Richmond

ROCKER REVIVAL

RED WOOL SWEATER, 1960S; ACRYLIC BSA SCARF, 1960S; STRETCH SKI-PANTS, EIDELWEISS, USA, 1960S; SHEEPSKIN-LINED VINYL ANKLE BOOTS, 1960S

UK 1978

Judy Westacott has worn these clothes since 1978, when she was 13 years old.

'I was an only child and almost continuously mixed with adults, many of whom had been rockers in the 1960s, and I was interested in their history' (Judy Westacott).

Worn and lent by **Judy Westacott**

FASHION ROCKER

BELLA FREUD (JACKET) AND PHILIP TREACY FOR BELLA FREUD (HAT)
UK *Spring/Summer 1994*

PINK WOOLLEN BOUCLÉ JACKET AND HAT
The jacket is based on the classic Perfecto jacket with its instantly recognizable diagonal zip. 'Traditionally a tough style but very accessible in fleecy little lamb pink. I like the idea of giving a very luxurious feel to a spare silhouette' (Bella Freud).   Given by Bella Freud

FASHION ROCKER JACKET AND HAT
PAM HOGG UK AUTUMN / WINTER 1988
Black leather jacket with metal studs and chains, PVC hat with metal studs

'For my *"Warrior Queen Collection"* I took Joan of Arc as my muse and offered interpretations of battle dress for women. Biker style was one of my sources'   *(Pam Hogg).*

ROCKER   UK MID-1960S
Black leather jacket customized with metal studs and chains, emblazoned with 'Rockers'; customized leather glove

Lent by **John Stuart**

Mod
Parka UK
early 1960s

50% nylon, 50% cotton,
silk-backed, uncut green wool parka,
shag lining, with 'American Army' patch, Vanderbilt
Shirt Company, USA, designed 1951, made April 1953
Parkas were practical, all-weather combat wear for the US
armed forces. By the early 1960s they were appropriated
by Mods as protective outer clothing while riding their
scooters. Ideally parkas had their original hoods
with fur trims and sometimes they were
customized with badges.

(Top) Mod Revival UK 1987-9

Charcoal and black striped wool
two-piece suit, Phil Segal, 'Italian
inspired', c.1960; cotton poplin shirt;
knitted silk tie, Dior; leather shoes

Italian-style tailored and casual wear was central
to Mods. This suit has a short, boxy 'bum freezer'
jacket with narrow lapels and cut-away fronts and
slim-line trousers with splits in the hems. It is
teamed with a horizontally striped tie and shirt
with tab collar. As a purist neo-Mod, Mike Ferrante,
calling himself a stylist, wore these clothes to
capture the original look.

Worn and lent by Mike Ferrante

(Bottom) Fashion Mod
Paul Smith
UK Autumn/Winter 1993

Brown and grey striped wool suit,
cotton shirt

Describing this suit from his 'True Brit' collection,
Paul Smith stated

'My inspiration came from the working class
Mods of the sixties who were influenced by the
eccentric Savile Row tailoring at the time.
It's the bringing together of the working and upper
classes through dressing that intrigues me.'

Boots given by Nicholas Deakins

(Right) Mod UK mid-1960s

Brown two-piece leather suit, Paul Blanche; nylon blouse with synthetic lace trim; canvas BOAC flight bag

Female Mods were characterized by their non body-conscious, almost androgynous appearance. Leather and suede were popular and Mod girls favoured A-line skirts with hems reaching just below the knee. BOAC and BEA flight bags, with their modernistic wing motifs, were desirable because of the travel connotations. The look was neat and streamlined and often completed by sensible 'granny style' shoes.

Compiled by Mike Ferrante

M O D

(Right) Mod UK mid-1960s

Black wool beret; knitted Courtelle shirt; black mohair trousers; corduroy shoes, Freeman Hardy & Willis

By the mid-1960s many Mods had moved on from the earlier smart suited look into more accessible, cheaper casual wear. Knitted shirts and berets were considered continental and progressive. Favourite footwear was often sand-coloured encompassing desert boots, Hush Puppies and corduroy lace-ups.

Compiled by Mike Ferrante

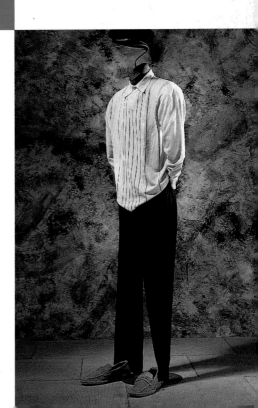

Hippy UK 1971

Blue patched denim jeans

Based in Carnaby Street,

Andrew Yiannakou constructed

these flared jeans by patching opened

denim waistbands together: there are 17

bands in each leg. Worn and given by Bob Langman

Hippy UK/American 1966. Linen suit and cotton shirt hand~painted by

'Saint', Mykonos, 1966; leather clogs Colin Woodhead was on the Greek island of Mykonos during 'the summer of love' in 1966. Here he met the American artist 'Saint' who was renowned for covering any surface with painted flowers. Colin Woodhead arranged to have his new linen suit (which he likened to a canvas) especially brought over from London to Mykonos and invited 'Saint' to adorn it. It is signed 'Saint~Amant'. The result is pure flower power~artistic expression of hippy style at its most refined. Worn and lent by Colin Woodhead

Hippy UK 1968. Afghan coat: block~printed viscose shirt. Indian: silk scarf. Indian: denim jeans. Wranglers. USA Afghan jerkins, jackets and coats were key items of hippy dress. Originally worn by Afghani shepherds, they are made from undyed skins, cured in urine, hand~embroidered and brought into Europe and America along the hippy Trail. This coat formerly belonged to the owner of the boutique Oxus, which retailed ethnic clothes and artifacts at World's End, Chelsea. Indian garments and leather sandals as well as denim jeans, which were often hand~patched and embroidered, also became mainstays of the hippy wardrobe. Worn and given by Peter Mendes

Fashion Hippy
Dolce & Gabanna

Italy, Spring/Summer 1993

Black cotton hat with multi~coloured feathers, patchwork trouser suit, silk blouse, patent leather platform sandals High fashion turned Hippy in the summer of 1993, and this stunning outfit received international media acclaim. The brightly coloured patchwork suit echoes the do-it-yourself ethos of the original 1960s Hippy look. Given by Dolce & Gabanna

Hippy UK/USA 1969. Multi~coloured, hand~ crochet wool hat and waistcoat, 'Think Sun', Birgitta Bjorke, USA; satin blouse, Ossie Clarke; assorted necklaces, Morocco; crepe trousers, Ossie Clarke; leather clogs This was one of Shirley Abicair's favourite outfits. At the time, she was a well known singer, TV presenter and a member of the Soho Arts Lab. She loved Ossie Clarke's clothes and combined them with special garments made by her creative friends. The stains on the trousers are historic ~ mud from Stonehenge! She sometimes painted her face with lace patterns in fluorescent colours when wearing this outfit. Worn and given by Shirley Abicair

PSYCHEDELIC

USA

1964

orange dress, cotton with fringing, sequins and ribbon, GRETCHEN 'FETCHIN' DOUGLAS; hand-painted boots (replicas)

Gretchen 'Fetchin' Douglas was a member of the Band of Merry Pranksters, who toured America in a painted school bus and played with The Grateful Dead in Ken Kesey's Acid Tests. She designed and made this outfit for herself and also made clothes for her friends. In eye-catching fluorescent colours, the dress and boots were intended to have maximum effect when she played the organ and performed in psychedelic light shows. This outfit was worn with a peacock feather headdress. Worn and lent by Gretchen 'Fetchin' Douglas

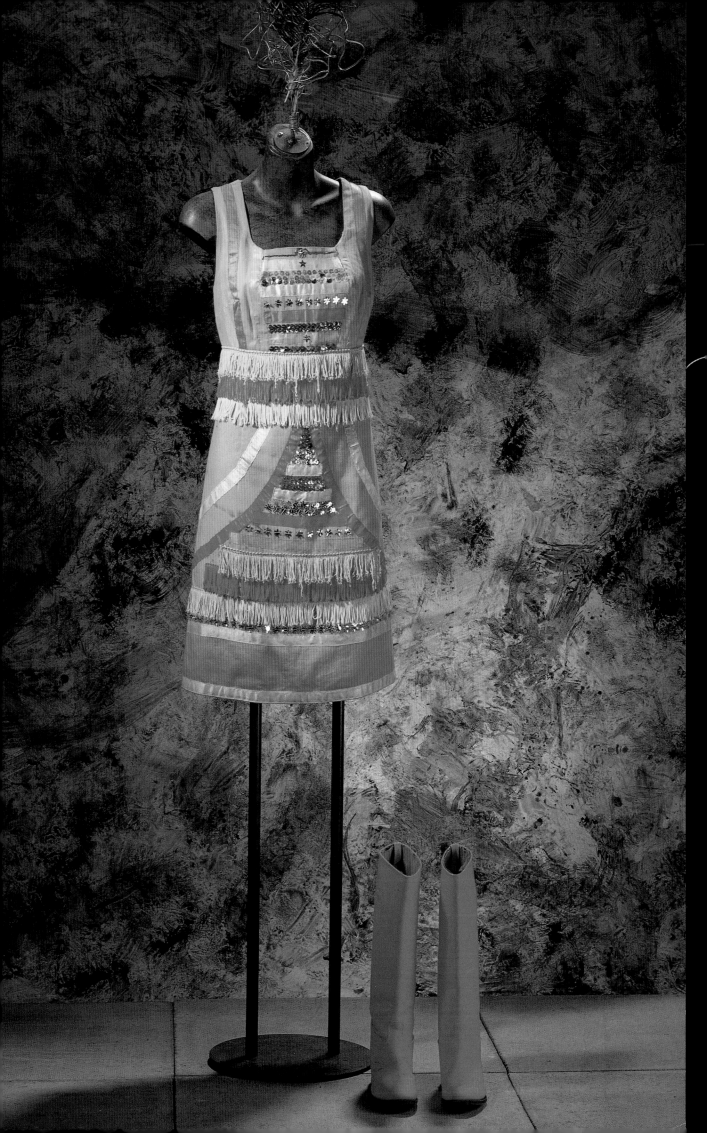

PSYCHEDELIC EDELIC UK c.1967

Red wool military jacket, ROYAL ENGINEERS, 1914; replica CND badge; voile shirt, MR FISH; striped cotton twill trousers; leather shoes.

Psychedelics appropriated Establishment attire and irreverently combined it with casual gear to achieve a contemporary peacock look. They donned jackets, often officers dress purchased from I Was Lord Kitchener's Valet (Portobello Road and then Carnaby Street) and adopted frilled dress shirts. Compiled by Andrew Yiannakou and Mike Ferrante

PSYCH EDELIC REVIVAL UK 1979

Black, gold and white synthetic brocade suit with Nehru jacket, ANDREW YIANNAKOU; crêpe-de-chine shirt, TURNBULL & ASSER, late 1960s

Andrew Yiannakou started to make psychedelic clothes in the late 1960s and was at the forefront of the revival in the early 1980s. He used 1960s patterns and original fabrics to create a purist revival style. At the end of 1979 he opened The Regal in Kensington Market. Clive Sutherland was a regular client who achieved an authentic look by combining Andrew Yiannakou's designs with period pieces. This suit was made to order. Given by Simon Harding in memory of Clive Sutherland. Worn by Clive Sutherland

RUDE BOY UK 1960S

Red felt hat;
Tonik suit, Haff
Tailors Ltd, UK;
cotton shirt,
National Sports
Shirts, Jamaica;
cotton string vest,
nylon socks USA;
leather loafers;
nylon underpants;
elastic braces;
silk handkerchief

'The Jamaicans were
famous for their loud
hats and their individually
tailored and extravagant
mixture of garments.
In Britain in the 1970s
we picked up on this
1960s style but stuck to
more low-key, off-the-peg
versions. The suit is
original 1960s but I
wore it in 1978 with as
much gold as we could
afford and we used gold
cigarette paper on our
teeth as a cap' (Gaz Mayall).

Worn by Gaz Mayall

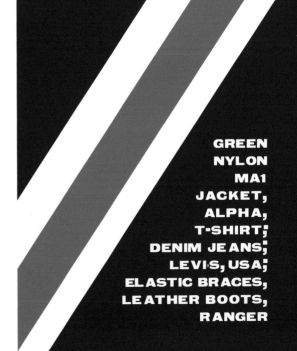

GREEN NYLON MA1 JACKET, ALPHA, T-SHIRT; DENIM JEANS; LEVI·S, USA; ELASTIC BRACES, LEATHER BOOTS, RANGER

SKINHEAD UK LATE 1980s

FROM 1978 PUNK STYLE FUSED WITH SKINHEAD TO CREATE A SCRUFFIER 'BONEHEAD' LOOK. BLEACHED ORANGE TAB LEVI'S WERE WORN BECAUSE OF THEIR NARROW CUT AND SKIN-TIGHT FIT, NEGATING THE NEED FOR BRACES, WHICH BECAME PURELY DECORATIVE AND WERE WORN HANGING DOWN. BOOTLACES WERE COLOUR CODED AND SLOGAN T-SHIRTS WERE WORN TO FLAUNT POLITICAL OR FOOTBALL TEAM AFFILIATIONS. IT WAS THIS LOOK THAT WAS APPROPRIATED BY SOME GAY MEN. WORN BY SHAUN COLE

SKINHEADS

SKINHEAD REVIVAL UK EARLY 1990S

GREEN/GOLD TWO PIECE TONIK SUIT; POLY-COTTON SHIRT; HOLEY 'MACKREL' NYLON TIGHTS; LEATHER LACE UP SHOES

THIS SUIT WAS MADE TO ORDER BY MMM TAILORING IN WALSALL AND COST £250. IT WAS MADE IN TONIK CLOTH, WHICH WAS MANUFACTURED EXCLUSIVELY BY DORMEUIL. 'I HAD IT ORIGINALLY TAILOR MADE, AS YOU CAN'T BUY THESE THREE-QUARTER LENGTH STYLE SUITS OFF-THE-PEG. THEY WERE WORN BY ORIGINAL-STYLE SKINHEAD GIRLS IN THE LATE 1960S AND EARLY 1970S. THEY WERE WORN MAINLY FOR BEST, FOR EVENING WEAR, DANCE HALLS. NOT A WORKING CLASS OUTFIT FOR DAILY USE,' (MANDY JARMAN). THIS LOOK IS CURRENTLY ENJOYING A REVIVAL AMONG A PURIST GROUP OF SKINHEADS.

WORN BY MANDY JARMAN

SKINHEAD UK EARLY 1970S

FAWN POLY-COTTON HARRINGTON JACKET, WRANGLER, USA, POLY-COTTON SHIRT, F.B: SLIM FIT, BLUE/GOLD TONIK TROUSERS, LEVI'S, USA, LEATHER BOOTS, DR MARTENS 1990S

WEARING TONIK TROUSERS AND A LIGHT-COLOURED HARINGTON JACKET OFFERED A SMART ALTERNATIVE TO THE LEVI'S DENIM TWO-PIECE. PICKING UP ON RUDE BOY STYLING, TROUSERS WERE WORN CROPPED TO SHOW THE TOPS OF THE BOOTS. FROM ABOUT 1970, PRINTED CHECKED FABRICS WERE THE MOST POPULAR CHOICE FOR SHIRTS. SKINHEADS APPROPRIATED HARRINGTON JACKETS, WHICH WERE WIDELY WORN FOR LEISURE AT THIS TIME.

COMPILED BY JONATHON HANNAH AND ELAINE GREEN

SKINHEAD UK 1971

BLUE DENIM JACKET, LEVI'S, USA; POLY-COTTON SHIRT, BRUTUS TRIMFIT; DENIM JEANS, LEVI'S, USA, ELASTIC BRACES; LEATHER BOOTS, DR MARTENS

JOHN G. BYRNE BECAME A SKINHEAD IN 1971 WHEN HE WAS JUST 12 YEARS OLD AND HAS RETAINED THE STYLE. HE STATES THAT

'IN MY OPINION SKINHEAD MEANS MORE THAN JUST A FASHION, IT'S A WHOLE LIFE.'

ALL THESE CLOTHES WERE BOUGHT IN BRIGHTON, AND HE CUSTOMISED THE JACKET BY INKING 'SKINS' ON THE BACK. AT THIS TIME THE SKINHEAD FORMULA WAS GINGHAM SHIRT, HALF-INCH WIDE BRACES AND STRAIGHT-CUT JEANS, LOOSER THAN THOSE WORN TODAY, WITH PRECISION TURN-UPS.

WORN BY JOHN G. BYRNE.

BROWN, GREEN, YELLOW AND RED CROCHET WOOL TAM; ARMY SURPLUS COTTON JACKET AND SHIRT, COTTON STRING VEST; COTTON TROUSERS; RAINBOW ELASTIC BRACES; NEWBUCK DECK SHOES

DURING THE 1970S THE MAINSTAYS OF THE RASTA'S WARDROBE WAS ARMY SURPLUS CLOTHES, COMBINED WITH GARMENTS IN THE DISTINCTIVE COLOURS OF THE ETHIOPIAN FLAG. GREEN REPRESENTS 'THE RICH LUXURIANT LAND THAT IS AFRICA'; GOLD 'THE WEALTH OF THE LAND'; AND RED 'THE ONE AND ONLY TRUE CHURCH' (HORACE CAMPBELL). NATURAL FIBRES WERE FAVOURED IN ACCORDANCE WITH ENVIRONMENTAL AND RELIGIOUS BELIEFS.

COMPILED BY DEREK FALCONER, CRAZY CLOTHES

RASTA UK 1970S

RASTA UK 1970S

BLACK, GREEN, YELLOW AND RED CROCHET
WOOL TAM; ARMY SURPLUS CAMOUFLAGE JACKET;
COTTON SHIRT; PRINTED COTTON T-SHIRT; ARMY
SURPLUS WOOL TROUSERS; NYLON BELT;
TERRACOTTA COCONUT AND RUBBER BONG;
ELASTIC TOWELLING SWEATBAND;
LEATHER BOOTS, ELLESSE

THE RASTA WOMEN IS FEMININE AND DEMURE IN HER APPEARANCE. SHE CLEARLY PROCLAIMS HER AFRICAN HERITAGE BY WEARING BATIKS DRAPED IN THE TRADITIONAL MANNER. THESE BATIKED TEXTILES WERE PRODUCED IN MANCHESTER FOR EXPORT TO THE AFRICAN MARKET AS WELL AS FOR DOMESTIC CONSUMPTION.

(TOP) FASHION RASTA
PHILIP TREACY FOR RIFAT OZBEK UK
SPRING/SUMMER 1991 (REMADE 1994)
PAMPAS GRASS MATTING PEAKED RASTA STYLE CAP

(BOTTOM) FASHION RASTA
MICHIKO KOSHINO UK
AUTUMN/WINTER 1993-4 (REMADE 1994)
WOOL HAT WITH TWEED DREADLOCKS

THE DREADS RASTA IS MORE MILITANT
AND THIS IS REFLECTED IN HIS DRESS. THE SURPLUS JACKET
WITH CAMOUFLAGE PRINT HAS OVERT MILITARISTIC CONNECTIONS.
THE T-SHIRT DESIGN FEATURES FLAGS OF AFRICAN NATIONS AND
AFRICAN NATIONALS TO PROMOTE THE DESIRE FOR THE REPATRIATION OF ALL
THEIR PEOPLES. GANGA, OTHERWISE KNOWN AS CANNABIS, IS AN INTEGRAL
PART OF RASTAFARIAN CULTURE, HENCE THE BONG IN HIS POCKET.
COMPILED BY DEREK FALCONER, CRAZY CLOTHES

RASTA UK C1980
COTTON BATIK HEAD WRAP;
PRINTED COTTON TOP;
LEATHER AND PAINT NECKLACE
COTTON BATIK SKIRT;
LEATHER SANDALS

WITH REFERENCE TO HIS RASTA COLLECTION, FOR WHICH PHILIP TREACY
WAS COMMISSIONED TO MAKE THE HATS, RIFAT OZBEK STATED 'I GOT MY INSPIRATION
FROM THE RASTAFARIANS IN NOTTING HILL GATE AND MIXED ELEMENTS
WITH HIGH TOPS TO MAKE IT MORE "STREETY". THE HAT WAS WORN WITH
STRETCH BODY SUITS IN 'RASTA' COLOURS. GIVEN BY PHILIP TREACY
'THIS HAT PROVIDES INSTANT FABRIC DREADLOCKS
FOR MAXIMUM IMPACT FOR THOSE WITH NO TIME TO GROW THEIR OWN'.
(MICHIKO KOSHINO) GIVEN BY MICHIKO KOSHINO

Funk

FUNK
US/USA
EARLY 1970s

Navy felt hat, Stately; patchwork leather coat, satin shirt, David Gordon; worsted flared trousers; patent-leather platform shoes, Ravel

It was the Black American pimp's style of dress, as promoted in film's like *Shaft* (1971) and *Superfly* (1972), that formed the basis of this look. The most outré and shiny 1970s fashions were combined with distinctive Funk items such as the patchwork leather trench coat, worn with a large felt hat.

The patent-leather platform shoes have purple heart motifs on the uppers.

Compiled by Derek Falconer, Crazy Clothes

FUNK
REVIVAL
UK 1993

White printed cotton T-shirt; soap stone and bone necklace;
original early 1970s denim patchwork jeans, Lee, USA;
leather platform shoes, USA.

'It was the perfect "funking" outfit to
wear at sweaty dives. A cross
between something old,
something futuristic and something wild,
something that
you could walk into a club with,
get your butt down and feel phat!'
(Emma Goodman).   Worn by Emma
Shoes given   Goodman
by Sarah
Callard.

GLAM

GLAM USA early 1970s

★ Blue & silver lamé top with silver lamé trim
★ Lamé trousers
★ Platform boots (re-painted silver)

Glam was a blatantly glitzy, futuristic, sexually-ambiguous style, which crossed over with American Funk and paved the way for the American and British disco scene.

Compiled by Derek Falconer, Crazy Clothes

FASHION GLAM Anthony Price UK 1973

★ Black & green sequinned silk jacket

'This was the beginning of Glam - the surface decoration draws on 1930s movie costumes and the cut is based on the classic Perfecto Rocker's jacket.' (Anthony Price)

Worn and lent by Bryan Ferry

GLAM UK early 1970s

★ Red feather boa
★ Printed T-shirt, 'Mr Freedom'
★ Velvet trousers
★ Ballet shoes

This look recalls the style of Marc Bolan, lead singer of T-Rex, who was a leading exponent of Glam style. These silvery-grey velvet trousers originally belonged to Bolan, who had made the transition from Mod to Hippy to Glam and often combined the latter two styles. He emphasized his petite frame by wearing ballet shoes in contrast to Glam's penchant for highly stacked platform shoes. Tommy Roberts opened his Mr Freedom boutique on the King's Road, Chelsea, in 1969, selling Glam, cutting-edge clothes, which are currently enjoying a revival.

Trousers worn by Marc Bolan, outfit compiled by Faebhean Kwest
Feather boa given by Revamp, Brighton
Trousers lent by Faebhean Kwest

NORTHERN SOUL

Silver-grey woollen suit, KEITH MALLINSON TAILORS; cotton shirt; black tie; cotton socks; leather brogues, 1994 based on 1970s originals, OFFICE SHOES • Jacket given by Peter Davies, Shoes given by Office Shoes, Suit worn by Peter Davies

'…people couldn't understand why their mates would go all this way when they weren't going to drink and they weren't going for the girls, so what was going on?' (Pete Rowe).

UK 1975

UK 1975
SOUTHERN SOUL

White cotton cap
sleeved T-shirt;
cotton gabardine
trousers, IMAGE & CO.

cotton bandanna;
plastic 'jellies' sandals

SANDALS LENT BY
REVAMP BRIGHTON
COMPILED BY JAY
STRONGMAN &
JO WALLACE

'Style was the name of the game and the Southern Soul/Funk scene was a reaction against the scruffy long hair and flairs then dominant in Britain. Many of the Soul club crowd were into David Bowie/Young Americans but went on to become members of the British Punk scene: plastic trousers, bin-liners and mohair jumpers were all first worn by this crowd' (Jay Strongman).

Soulies took elements from mid-1960s Mod suits and 1970s football styles. Trousers with exaggerated flares were cut short to prevent tripping, as it was vital that garments should allow free movement for dancing. The suits could not be bought off the peg and had to be custom-made - each client dictating the positions of numerous pockets and buttons. All-nighters and all-dayers, the forerunners of raves, were held at clubs such as Wigan Casino.

AT THE PEAK OF THE NORTHERN SOUL SCENE KEITH MALLINSON IN ROTHERHAM WAS MAKING 150 PAIRS OF SOUL TROUSERS A WEEK.

IN THE FOLLOWING FIVE YEARS MOST PEOPLE HAD THE FLARES ALTERED, WHICH ACCOUNTS FOR THEIR SCARCITY TODAY.

Keith Mallinson has retained the original pattern and re-made the trousers.

---

early 1970s

These clothes were worn by Derek Falconer, who bought them in Shaftesbury Avenue, in the early 1970s. This is a distinctive Soul Boy look which was popularized by pop stars, including Errol Brown, lead singer of Hot Chocolate, and Isaac Hayes, who wrote the musical score for the 1971 film Shaft.

UK / USA

Leather cap (re-made by owner 1994; leather waistcoat, Trailmaster USA; leather trousers, Silton, USA; leather platform shoes, UK. Worn by Derek Falconer, Crazy Clothes

Skater UK 1992-3

TM

Grey cotton shirt, Ben Davis, USA; cotton T-shirt, Consolidated, USA; cotton and plastic hat, A1 Meats, USA; cotton pants, Fuct, USA; suede trainers, Vans Half Cabs Caberlleros, USA.

1992 saw skateboard wear at its 'fattest', paralleling Hip Hop styles. Every garment had to be XL, XXL or XXXL and customized to the owner's design. The £60.00 trainers have been cut-down from hightops, sealed with stickers, and 'shoe goo' has been applied to protect the sides. This T-shirt was worn inside out as the logo was no longer 'cool' and the £75.00 'fat' pants hung low with the bottoms cut and frayed. Compiled by Slam City Skates

Snowboarder UK 1994

Blue jacket, Twist and Morrow, Australia; pants, Westbeach Outland, Australia; T-shirt, fleece beanie hat, 'Hoodah' pullover, Low Pressure; leather boots

Since the late 1970s sportswear has been appropriated by many subcultural groups. This outfit represents an increasing interest in the sport of snowbording, which is becoming more and more evident on the street. It is a combination of skiwear and surf/skatewear using new technology winter fabrics. Many of the original surf clothing companies now produce snowbording garments using recycled plastic and eco-friendly cotton. Compiled by Low Pressure

PUNK UK/USA

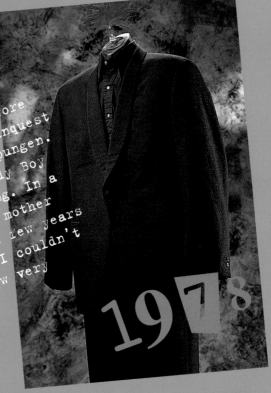

1978

These clothes were purchased by Sid Vicious, the Sex Pistols' bass guitarist, in New York. He wore them for formal occasions, including the inquest into the death of his girlfriend, Nancy Spungen. The jacket shows the influence of the Teddy Boy drape and the shirt draws on Western styling. In a letter authenticating these clothes, Sid's mother wrote, 'I hadn't seen Sid in a suit for a few years and despite the sadness of the occasion, I couldn't help thinking as he walked towards us, how very imposing he looked.' Worn by Sid Vicious

Lent by Christopher Moore

FASHION PUNK

ZANDRA RHODES

UK

1977

'Punk was in the air. She set to work making aesthetic holes in silk jersey and beading safety pins. And Lo! A collection of tattered couture dresses' (Zandra Rhodes quoted in *The Observer*, 9 October 1977). This best-selling sheath dress was from Zandra Rhodes's controversial 'Conceptual Chic' Collection. Given by Zandra Rhodes

PUNK UK 1977

GREEN-BLACK NYLON SHIRT WITH

'GOD SAVE THE QUEEN' PATCH

'VIVE LE ROCK'

T-SHIRT, COTTON TROUSERS

WITH BONDAGE STRAPS

STRIPED MOHAIR JUMPER,

LEATHER SLING BACK SHOES

Like striped mohair jumpers, T-shirts with irreverent and confrontational slogans were central to Punk style. Bondage trousers with bum flaps, zips and straps were first retailed by Westwood and McLaren in September 1976, and represented a development from the leather bondage clothes sold in their previous shop 'Sex'. When George Slattery bought these clothes he was aged 17 and working as a printer's apprentice. The jumper cost £25.

Worn by George Slattery

SEDITIONAIRES

VIVIENNE WESTWOOD

AND MALCOLM McLAREN

PUNK UK

1976-77

CUSTOMIZED WHITE
COTTON SHIRT;
ZIPPED COTTON T-SHIRT;
COTTON TROUSERS; LEATHER SHOES
AND PLASTIC 'JELLIES' SANDALS

Christine Powell created
a low-cost Punk look by
customizing existing garments.
She transformed a man's
collarless shirt by splattering
it with paint, slashing the fabric
and securing it with chains and
safety pins. The lower left front is
inscribed 'Vicious'. The trousers
were originally an early 1970s skirt
which she remade into drainpipe trousers.
In the evening she wore this outfit
with white stiletto shoes and during
the day with flat 'jelly' plastic sandals.
Worn by Christine Powell.

BLACK COTTON JACKET, BOY;

DYED AND CUT-UP STRING VESTS;

SKULL AND CROSSBONE BOOTLACE TIE;

COTTON TROUSERS, SEDITIONAIRES;

LEATHER WORK BOOTS WITH STEEL TOECAPS

PUNK

UK 1976

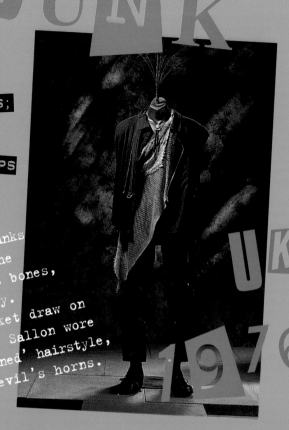

Punk style
leader Philip Sallon
combined 'Seditionaries' clothes
with personalized items, such as the cut-up
and painted string vests seen here. To the
immense irritation of many Teddy Boys, some Punks
appropriated items of Ted style, such as the
bootlace tie – this one has a skull and cross bones,
appealing to the anarchic Punk sensibility.
In nihilistic black, the trousers and jacket draw on
combat gear. To add further impact, Philip Sallon wore
heavy black eye make-up and a striking 'horned' hairstyle,
which he likens to a Viking helmet or devil's horns.

Worn and given by Philip Sallon

FASHION PUNK UK
DAVID SHILLING
(RE-MADE 1994)

BLACK SEQUINS

AND OSTRICH FEATHERS

'Street fashion is for people with more
time than money and haute couture is
for people with lots of money. I wanted
to give someone who could afford to buy
it the opportunity to experience the
excitement of Punk, without any of the
headaches!!!' (David Shilling).
While showing this hat, which was inspired by
the mohican hairstyle adopted by many Punks,
the model wore a black plastic bin-liner.
Given by David Shilling

1980

NEW

New·Romantic
Kahn & Bell
UK ·1980~1
(re~made 1993)

Jewelled gold kid leather,
black silk and Lycra outfit:
crowned helmet, skirt, collar, choker,
cloak with bells, bodice, belt,
gauntlet mittens, body, leggings,
wedge-soled boots, earrings

Jane Kahn and partner
Patty Bell had the shop
'Kahniverous' in the Great Gear
Market, Kings Road, Chelsea.
Their design sources were eclectic,
embracing the arts of Egypt, Africa
and the Far East, which they
combined with notes of futurism
and pure fantasy. Their elaborate,
almost theatrical styles had a
particular appeal to the more extreme
New Romantics.

'STAGE' NEW-ROMANTIC VIVIENNE WESTWOOD·UK 1982

Black wool tail coat with gold buttons & braiding Lurex ruffled shirt with cotton stock and jabot
tricolour cotton sash ≈ leather belt ≈ silver leather breeches ≈ leather riding boots

Pop singer Adam Ant wore this many~layered outfit in performance for his 'Prince Charming'
tour and on the album's cover. Like his previous pirate persona, the highwayman cut a dashing,
heroic figure, which had long been glorified in literature and Hollywood films. These elaborate clothes
resembled costumes worn to New Romantic clubs.

Lent by The Theatre Museum ≈ Worn and given by Adam Ant

RØMANTIC

NEW RØMANTIC·UK·1979

Black tricorn hat ≈ Green wool frock coat
Cotton shirt & jabot ≈ Corduroy breeches

After the aggressive overtones of Punk,
Philip Sallon revelled in the unashamed
foppishness and decadence of
New Romanticism. Inspiration was
derived from fictional heroes & villains,
historicism and futuristic sources.
In creating this outfit, Philip's desire was
to achieve an 18th~Century flamboyance by
assembling a range of new and reproduction
clothing. He wore these with silk stockings
and Chinese sandals, with the straps under
his feet to resemble 18th~Century shoes.
Hiring period costume and fancy dress was
in vogue, resulting in a blatant masquerade.

Worn and lent by Philip Sallon

Glam Rocker

HEAD BANGER UK LATE 1970s

Red leather jacket; cotton T-shirt,
KISS 1980 ; Spandex trousers,
JEAN ELLE, GLENDRA, USA;
studded leather belt; metal rings
and chains; leather cowboy boots

This body-conscious outfit reveals the
influences of Cowboy (1940), Rocker
(1950) and Glam Disco (1970) styles
and appeals to the more glamorous
followers of Heavy Metal music.
It is a mix of overt masculinity with
feminine overtones. A red leather
jacket replaces the customary black
leather Rocker-style jacket and is
worn over the essential tour T-shirt,
featuring the Glam Rock band Kiss.
Pseudo-Satanism is featured on logos
and jewellery and is worn by a number
of subcultures including Glam
Rockers, Headbangers and Goths.

Compiled by Kate Webb, Morticia

Ted Nugent

SCORPIONS

RUSH 2112

AC/DC
HIGHWAY TO HELL

RUSH

LET THERE BE ROCK
AC/DC

Head
BANGER

UK 1980

SCORPIONS

SCS
ARMED AND READY
TOUR 1980

VAN HALEN
VAN HALEN

Denim patched jacket; cotton STATUS QUO T-shirt; denim jeans; leather belt; leather hightop trainers; boot straps

Headbangers and Heavy Metal heads share a similar taste in music, though their clothing can be very different. Like Rockers, Headbangers' clothes are celebrated for being distressed and rarely clean. Layers of jeans, patched and embroidered jackets, plus tour T-shirts are the norm. This look has evolved from the Hippies and original Californian Hells Angels styles of the 1960s.

T-shirt given by Kate Webb

PSYCHOBILLY UK 1980s

CUSTOMIZED BLACK
LEATHER JACKET
PRINTED METEORS T-SHIRT
PATCHED AND
RIPPED DENIM JEANS
LEVI'S, USA
STUDDED LEATHER
BELT AND LEATHER
KNIFE POUCH
DR MARTENS
BOOTS WITH
STUDDED STRAP

THE DISTINCTIVELY PSYCHOBILLY PAINTED LEATHER JACKET INCORPORATES MOTIFS AND LETTERING USED ON THE METEORS AND THE CRAMPS ALBUM COVERS. SIMILAR WORDING HAS BEEN INKED ON THE JEANS. SLEEVES WERE RIPPED OFF T-SHIRTS TO REVEAL ELABORATELY TATTOOED BODIES. THE PUNK INFLUENCE ON PSYCHOBILLY STYLE IS SEEN HERE IN THE RIPPED JEANS WITH TARTAN PATCHES AND THE STUDDED BELT. FAKE FUR PATCHES AND HEAVY 'DIRTBOX' STYLE BOOTS REVEAL THE ROCKABILLY LINK.

COMPILED BY JUDY WESTACOTT IN CONJUNCTION WITH RAY HARE, JO DE CASTRO AND SHAUN JOHN

LENT BY RAY HARE, JO DE CASTRO AND SHAUN JOHN

FASHION CASUAL ©

VIVIENNE WESTWOOD

UK 1984

Printed nylon stretch body-suit with appliqué patches

Worn as gay club wear, the surface decoration of this bodysuit reinforces the advertising imagery of the football stadium - the home of the Casual. Its colouring and stripes draw on football-players kit.

Worn by Rupert Michael Dolan. Given by David Barber in memory of Rupert Michael Dolan

CASUALS PERRY UK c1978

Navy blue cagoule, Adidas; wool jumper, Pringle; cotton T-shirt, Fred Perry; jumbo cords, Lois, Spain; leather shoes, Pods, 1994 based on 1970s originals

'Perries saw themselves as rivals to neo-Mods and were smart and clean cut in rebellion against the scruffy Punk image' (Simon Connell). Perries nearly always wore Fred Perry T-shirts, hence their name, and they were one of the first recognizable groups to clothe themselves in sportswear from head to toe. The labels eventually became more important than the style of the clothes.

Cagoule given by Alan McFarlane
T-shirt given by Fred Perry
Trousers given by Shaun Turpin
Shoes given by Pods
Jumper given by Simon Attwood

CASUALS

CASUALS UK 1982-4

White polyester and cotton tracksuit top, Sergio Tacchini, Italy; cotton shirt, Lacoste, Italy; lambswool jumper, Pringle; bleached denim jeans, Lee, USA; leather trainers, Bjorn Borg Diadoras, Italy; fake Rolex watch

A later manifestation of the Casual style, this look was based on an assembly of pastel-coloured leisure and sportswear with international brand names. Casuals were devoted to expensive labels which were changed continually in order that rival factions might 'out cool' each other. A particular fad was to customize jeans by removing the machined hems, splitting the side seams and fraying the raw edges.

Worn by Justin Alphonse

FASHION CASUAL
KATHARINE HAMNETT UK
SPRING/SUMMER 1994

Grey, black and yellow cotton bobble hat, cotton jersey tracksuit, cotton scarf; leather sandals, Birkenstocks, Germany

Football supporter style has been translated by Katharine Hamnett into a carefully co-ordinated casual outfit. She describes it as 'The alternative World Cup Special'.

Given by Katharine Hamnett Shoes given by the Natural Shoe Store

CASUALS UK 1994

Red rubberized cotton jacket; woollen hat; acrylic fleece sweatshirt, Gio Goi; sweatshirt, Sabotage; denim jeans, Chipie, France; deck shoes, Ralph Lauren, USA

After a brief dalliance with the Rave scene, Casuals re-appeared as a recognizable group on the football terraces in the early 1990s. The directors of Gio Goi were themselves Casuals and built up an international clothing company based around this look. The preoccupation with labels remained: favourites were now Chevignon, Stone Island, Naf Naf, Diesel and Ralph Lauren.

Jeans given by Chipie Deck shoes given by Office Shoes

OLD SKOOL
B-BOY
UK c1985

**BLACK LEATHER
GOOSE-DOWN JACKET,**
DOUBLE GOOSE DOWN, USA;
COTTON TOWELLING BERMUDA
CASUAL HAT, KANGOL;
COTTON 'RUN-DMC' SWEATSHIRT,
LEATHER TRACKSUIT TROUSERS,
LEATHER TRAINERS,
ADIDAS, UK;
GOLD NECK CHAIN

WORN AND LENT BY STEVE PANG

I WAS 14 AND LIVING IN BRISTOL WHEN I FIRST BECAME INTERESTED IN BEING A B-BOY. I WAS WATCHING KIDS RAPPING BUT THEY WERE CONFUSED BECAUSE THEY WERE WEARING CASUAL CLOTHES AND RAPPING TO HIP-HOP I WAS GETTING INTO THE CLOTHES BECAUSE OF THE LABELS. IT SEEMS AS THOUGH EVERYTHING AMERICAN WAS THE MOST DESIRABLE. EVERYONE WANTED KANGOL HATS AND PUMA STATES - NO MATTER HOW STUPID THEY LOOKED. BASICALLY IT WAS MORE CREDIBLE IF YOU COULDN'T BUY IT OFF THE SHELF.

FASHION B-BOY/FLY GIRL
KARL LAGERFELD
FOR CHANEL
FRANCE SPRING/SUMMER 1994

FLUORESCENT PINK LYCRA
TWO-PIECE BRA-TOP,
DENIM SHORTS WITH BRACES,
CANVAS BOOTS

CHANEL S DESIGNER KARL LAGERFELD IS FRIENDS WITH THE AFROCENTRIC RAP BAND ARRESTED DEVELOPMENT AND HIS B-BOY/FLY GIRL INFLUENCES HAVE THUS BEEN IMBUED AT FIRST HAND. THE BAGGY SHORTS ARE PICKED UP FROM B-BOYS AND THE BRA-TOP DRAWS ON FLY GIRL AND RAGGA SOURCES.

GIVEN BY CHANEL

OLD SKOOL
B-BOY
UK/USA 1982

BLUE COTTON BASEBALL CAP,
SUGAR HILL RECORD LABEL;
COTTON 'WILDSTYLE'
T-SHIRT, ZEPHYR; COTTON JEANS;
LEATHER TRAINERS, ADIDAS CENTURY;
'FAT' LACES

CHARACTERIZED BY THE LIBERAL USE OF ADIDAS SPORTSWEAR - BASEBALL HATS, JACKETS AND TRAINERS WITH *FAT* LACES - THE OLD SKOOL LOOK HAS BECOME A CLASSIC, REWORKED BY MANY SUBCULTURES SINCE THE LATE 1980S. THE *WILDSTYLE* T-SHIRT REFLECTS THE MAJOR PART GRAFFITI HAS PLAYED IN HIP HOP CULTURE. DESIGNED BY THE NEW YORK BASED GRAFFITI ARTIST ZEPHYR, THE SHIRT WAS PRINTED FOR THE JAPANESE PREMIERE OF THE HIP HOP FILM *WILDSTYLE* IN 1982.

T-SHIRT GIVEN BY ALISON NOVAK TROUSERS, TRAINERS AND HAT LENT BY STEVE PANG

COMPILED BY STEVE PANG

BROWN LEATHER
AND NYLON TRACKSUIT,
FAKE GUCCI PRINT;
LEATHER AND PLASTIC
BASEBALL HAT, FAKE FENDI;
PLASTIC AND
LEATHER BUMBAG,
FAKE LOUIS VUITTON PRINT;
GOLD METAL DOLLAR PENDANT;
LEATHER TRAINERS,
NIKE AIR FLIGHT;
SUN-GLASSES

BRAND CONSCIOUSNESS AND RELENTLESS COMPETITION AMONGST HIP HOPPERS, IN THE MID TO LATE 1980S, EVENTUALLY LED TO INDIVIDUAL CUSTOMIZATION. TAILORS, THE MOST FAMOUS BEING DAPPER DAN IN HARLEM, NEW YORK, TOOK THE MOST EXPENSIVE AND CONSERVATIVE DESIGNS OF COVETED LABELS AND ADDED AN EXTRA TWIST OF 'STREET FLAVOUR'. HERE THE TRACKSUIT, ALWAYS A POPULAR GARMENT FOR B-BOYS, WAS DESIGNED IN WHAT BECAME KNOWN AS 'GHETTO COUTURE' WITH FAKE GUCCI, FENDI AND LOUIS VUITTON PRINTS.

COMPILED BY NORMSKI AND FOUR STAR GENERAL
TRAINERS LENT BY STEVE PANG

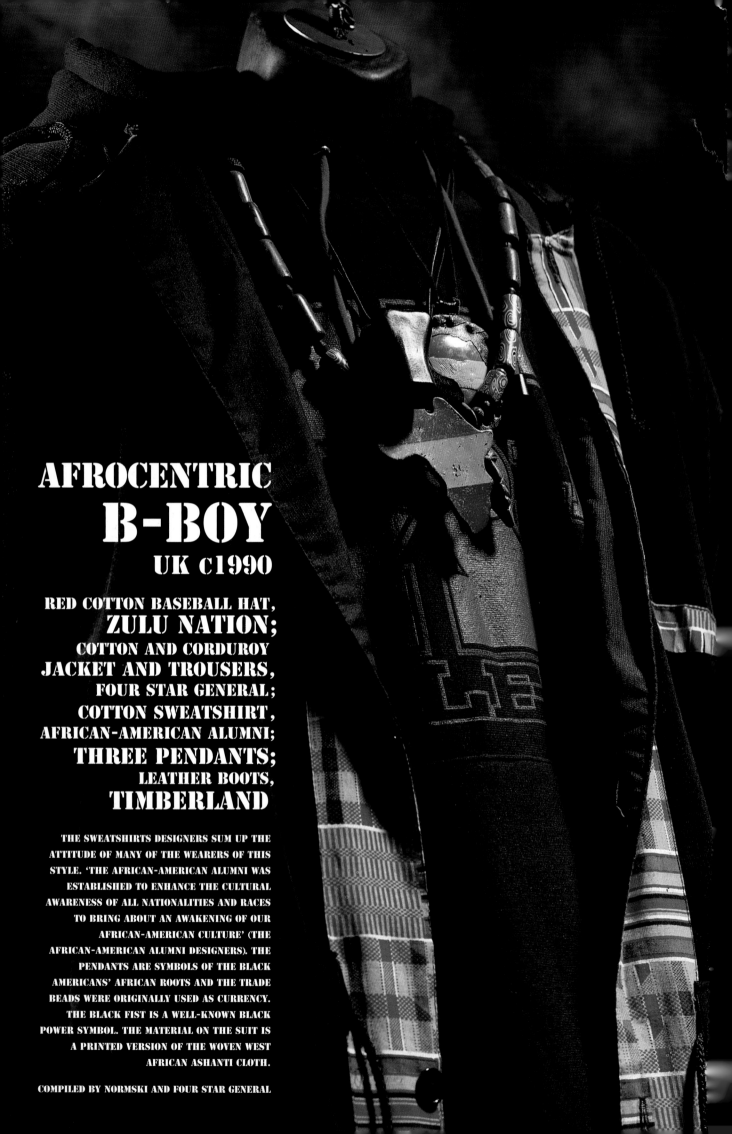

AFROCENTRIC
B-BOY
UK c1990

RED COTTON BASEBALL HAT,
ZULU NATION;
COTTON AND CORDUROY
JACKET AND TROUSERS,
FOUR STAR GENERAL;
COTTON SWEATSHIRT,
AFRICAN-AMERICAN ALUMNI;
THREE PENDANTS;
LEATHER BOOTS,
TIMBERLAND

THE SWEATSHIRTS DESIGNERS SUM UP THE
ATTITUDE OF MANY OF THE WEARERS OF THIS
STYLE. 'THE AFRICAN-AMERICAN ALUMNI WAS
ESTABLISHED TO ENHANCE THE CULTURAL
AWARENESS OF ALL NATIONALITIES AND RACES
TO BRING ABOUT AN AWAKENING OF OUR
AFRICAN-AMERICAN CULTURE' (THE
AFRICAN-AMERICAN ALUMNI DESIGNERS). THE
PENDANTS ARE SYMBOLS OF THE BLACK
AMERICANS' AFRICAN ROOTS AND THE TRADE
BEADS WERE ORIGINALLY USED AS CURRENCY.
THE BLACK FIST IS A WELL-KNOWN BLACK
POWER SYMBOL. THE MATERIAL ON THE SUIT IS
A PRINTED VERSION OF THE WOVEN WEST
AFRICAN ASHANTI CLOTH.

COMPILED BY NORMSKI AND FOUR STAR GENERAL

MILITARY-PE
B-BOY
UK 1988

**BLACK AND GREY COTTON
NATO ARCTIC CAMOUFLAGE
JACKET AND TROUSERS;**

BASEBALL HAT,

COTTON T-SHIRT,

PUBLIC ENEMY;

LEATHER HOLSTER;

METAL BELT BUCKLE,

LEATHER ARMY BOOTS,

FOUR STAR GENERAL

IN THE LATE 1980S THE BLACK MILITANT LOOK
WAS EPITOMIZED BY THE BAND PUBLIC ENEMY.
ON THEIR FIRST LP, 'YO! BUM RUSH THE SHOW'
RELEASED IN 1987, THEY WERE DRESSED IN
ARMY CAMOUFLAGE, BLACK BERETS AND
HOLDING UZIS. THIS LOOK BECAME POPULAR AS
AN EXPRESSION OF BLACK CONSCIOUSNESS.
EVERY CONCEIVABLE GARMENT WAS
EMBLAZONED WITH THE SILHOUETTE AND
CROSS-WIRE LOGO OF PUBLIC ENEMY.

COMPILED BY NORMSKI AND FOUR STAR GENERAL

Prince of Wales check / Glen Plaid Trevira
dress; leather loafers, Bass Weejuns

"This 1971 Skinhead dress was given to me
in 1978 by a 27-year-old friend. She gave it to
me on the understanding that it was going to a
safe place. I immediately had the spoonbill
collar altered to its present button down form.
The length was perfect — I didn't want it to
show under my Tonik combie. I wore Bass
Weejun loafers (they had to be Oxblood) and
white holey mackerel tights." (Jo Wallace)

Worn by Jo Wallace

TWO TONE [UK c1978]
Black felt porkpie hat; cotton customized jacket, Harrington;
cotton T-shirt, Fred Perry; cotton trousers, Brutus Sta Press;
leather loafers; Wayfarer sun-glasses, Ray-Ban

1960s West Indian Rude Boy clothing was updated by the
neo-Mods and Skinheads of the late 1970s to form Two Tone;
the outcome is clearly evident in this outfit. The characteristic
black and white combination, checkerboard patterning and
badges celebrated the multi-cultural mix of the band members
as well as their music.

Jacket lent by Stuart Harrison
T-shirt given by Fred Perry
Sun-glasses given by Clare Browne
Trousers lent by Mike Ferrante

TWO TONE [UK 1979]
Bronze and turquoise wool Tonik suit, 1960s;
cotton shirt, Ben Sherman; cotton towelling
sports socks; leather loafers; wool blue beat hat

Jerry Dammers was one of the chief agents in
the promotion of the Two Tone look. As founder
of The Specials, 2 Tone record label, and as a
graphic artist, he was mainly responsible for
the distinctive black and white Two Tone image.
He discovered this 1960s single-breasted Mod
suit in a second hand shop which promptly led
to the look being picked up by subsequent Two
Tone bands and their fans.

Shirt lent by Shaun Cole
Worn by Jerry Dammers

xx**FETISH**xx

UK 1986

Black rubber jacket,
rubber trousers, Ectomorph;
leather boots, Dr Martens

xxxxxxxxxxxxxxxxxxxxxx

BOOTS GIVEN BY DR MARTENS
Jacket and trousers given by Ectomorph

Here, a basic MOTORBIKE-STYLE jacket and jeans
are transformed by the use of LATEX. ECTOMORPH
was one of the first to popularize RUBBER clothing.
Owner KRYSTINA KITSIS'S aim was to 'FUSE
FETISHISM WITH SOPHISTICATED FASHION'.
✳ THE KEY TO HER APPROACH WAS TO TREAT
RUBBER AS SHE MIGHT ANY OTHER FABRIC. ✳

FETISH

UK 1994

BLACK FISHNET BODY STOCKING,
LEATHER CHAPS, LEATHER GLADIATOR COLLAR.
LEATHER HARNESS, LEATHER POUCH,
LEATHER GLOVES, LEATHER CAP, LEATHER PURSE.
LEATHER THONG, LIZ LEWITT FOR RELIGION.
LEATHER BIKER BOOTS, SHELLYS

'IT COMES BACK TO THE WAY THE
BRITISH ARE ABOUT SEX AND ABOUT
FORMS OF EXPRESSION. THEY ALWAYS
SEE ANYTHING LIKE THIS AS BEING REALLY
SMUTTY, SEEDY AND DISTASTEFUL
WHEREAS TO ME ITS JUST PART OF
CLOTHING'   (LIZ LEWITT).

This outfit is intentionally genderless,   Boots given
breaking the stereotypes of Fetish clothing.   by Shellys
It draws heavily on Western, B-Boy and Gay styles   Outfit compiled
and has influenced the female Ragga look.   by Liz Lewitt

FASHION FETISH
PAM HOGG
UK 1989

GOLD LEATHER STRAPPY OUTFIT WITH SEPARATE ANKLE.
WRIST AND NECK CUFFS, COTTON AND LYCRA KNICKERS.
PATENT LEATHER STILETTO-HEELED ANKLE BOOTS

'ANGELIC BONDAGE.'
Pam Hogg is especially well known
for her FETISHISTIC CLUB
CLOTHES. This outfit is from her
BRAVE NEW WORLD COLLECTION.
'I GAVE THE BOOTS A LITTLE PLATFORM TO
MAKE THEM LESS PAINFUL TO WALK IN'
(Pam Hogg).

LENT BY PAM HOGG

GOTHური 1986

Black chiffon cape
lace-trimmed velveteen top;
fringed velveteen skirt;
lace mittens;
studded leather belts;
nylon lace tights;
buckled-leather boots.

" The wearer states that the appeal of this look was

"..... it's unusual, extravagant and ghostly, which
reflected my interests in the mysterious. At the
same time, it's feminine, dressy, style involved
big hair, lots of make-up and jewellery.
It was like wearing fancy dress." [Sechnaz Hussan]

The clothes were bought from Camden Market
and Oasis in Birmingham and were then customized.

Worn by Sehnaz Hussan.

Goth 1984

Black wool coat; silky shirt with jabot;
silk velvet waistcoat; worsted trousers;
leather boots, La Grande Botte, Mexico;

Dave Vanian was the lead singer of the cult Goth band The Damned
and he represented the ultimate in Goth style. His wife, laurie, ran the
influential Goth clothing shop called Symphony of Shadows, London,
and made the clothes he wore on and off stage. Dramatic and
sometimes sinister, black and purple dominated and fed the Goth's
preoccupation with death and mourning.

Worn and lent by Dave Vanian

Matt Black Minimal	UK	1984 - 88
Black cotton polo-neck, Gap; denim jeans, Levi's 501's, USA; rubber belt; leather shoes, Toro; nylon portfolio, Junior Gaultier; Ray-ban sunglasses.	'During the 1980s black was the strongest, longest fashion colour, both within the business and on the high street. This extended to accessories and within the home'	
Worn by Tony Glenville		

COMPILED BY DEREK FALCONER, CRAZY CLOTHES

YARDIE JAMAICA 1980S

KHAKI COTTON SHIRT

STRING VEST
COTTON TWILL
TROUSERS
LEATHER SHOES

SOME YOUNG JAMAICANS DID **MILITARY SERVICE IN CASTRO'S CUBA.** ON RETURNING TO JAMAICA THEY WERE COMFORTABLE IN CLOTHES WHICH STILL HAD MILITARY OVERTONES.

YARDIE UK EARLY 1980S
BLACK HAT, KANGOL; WOOL CARDIGAN WITH SUEDE TRIM, GABICCI, ITALIAN; SILK SHIRT; GOLD METAL NECKLACE WITH NEFERTITI HEAD PENDANT; CRIMPLENE TROUSERS, FARAH; LEATHER SHOES, BALLY
THE BRITISH YARDIE'S CLOTHING IS SMART AND BODY AND LABEL CONSCIOUS. DESIRABLE AND MUCH WORN ITEMS INCLUDE FARAH TROUSERS, GABICCI CARDIGANS, 'YARDIE CARDIES', AND SHOES BY BALLY AND PIERRE CARDIN. JEWELLERY WAS CENTRAL TO THE STYLE, AND THICK GOLD ROPE CHAINS WITH NEFERTITI HEADS, CANNABIS LEAVES, ONYX MEDALLIONS AND SOVEREIGNS WERE FAVOURITE PIECES. TROUSERS GIVEN BY FARAH
COMPILED WITH THE ADVICE OF THE V&A'S SECURITY STAFF

FASHION YARDIE
THE DUFFER OF ST GEORGE
UK AUTUMN/WINTER 1993
BLACK, RED AND WHITE 'YARDIE CARDIE', PRINTED COTTON JERSEY T-SHIRT, WORSTED TROUSERS, SUEDE BOOTS
'THE INFLUENCE CAME FROM THE LATE 1960S/EARLY 1970S REGGAE/YARDIE SCENE BUT ALSO HAD MANY OTHER STYLISTIC REFERENCES, I.E. EARLY SIXTIES ITALIAN, BEATNIK AND, MORE SUBTLY, LATE SEVENTIES FOOTBALL CASUAL. THIS IN ESSENCE WAS THE REASON FOR ITS SUCCESS - THE MULTITUDE OF MEANINGS TO MANY DIFFERENT TYPES OF PEOPLE' (THE DUFFER OF ST GEORGE). GIVEN BY THE DUFFER OF ST GEORGE

YARDIE JAMAICA 1980S
GOLD LUREX DRESS AND LEATHER BOOTS
IT IS NOT UNUSUAL FOR YARDIE GIRLS TO CHANGE SEVERAL TIMES A DAY FROM ONE EYE-CATCHING OUTFIT TO ANOTHER, ALWAYS WORN WITH GREAT PANACHE AND TONS OF JEWELLERY.
COMPILED BY DEREK FALCONER, CRAZY CLOTHES

INDIE UK 1988

Brown jacket, ARMY   SURPLUS;
 knitted acrylic cardi-
gan and   cotton and elastane
leggings,
MARKS & SPENCER;
 cotton T- shirt, CONCEPT MAN;

hand-embroidered Indian skirt,
MISS SELFRIDGE;
leather boots, DR   MARTENS;
 cotton laces;
 jewellery

'I wanted a distinct look that cost very little, the altern- ative was to buy cheap chainstore clothes and look like a "**Sharon**" ' (Lucie Dingwall).

Although the garments were worn as an outfit in 1988, due to a shortage of money they had been acquired gradually over a number of years from various sources. The skirt (1986), originally long and full, was customized in early 1988 and the cardigan (1985) was the result of a swap between cousins.

Worn and given by Lucie Dingwall
Boots given by Revamp, Brighton
T-shirt given by Sarah Callard

INDIE UK 1984

Brown suede and wool cardigan, MARKS & SPENCER;
cotton T-shirt, THE SMITHS;
denim jeans, LEVI'S, USA;
leather shoes, DR MARTENS

Here, inspiration is taken from 1950s design and fashion trends. Coming at the end of the neo-Rockabilly movement (1978 82), this look was popularized by the influential band **The Smiths**. The Indie style, incorporating **Dr Martens**, band T shirts and cheap second-hand clothing, became a uniform for many students in the 1980s and 90s.

T-shirt given by Roger Kite
Shoes given by Revamp, Brighton

Traveller UK, 1989-93

Fraggle is a member of the Donga Tribe, who travels and campaigns to save the enviroment. A composition of bright layers of second-hands and customized clothings provides the colourful and unkempt look. The hand-made socks, crafted accessories and ethnic Indian waistcoat, display a sympathy towards other cultures and a preference for a self-sufficient lifestyle. The dress was made by owner for her first festival. "I was run over by a bulldozer in this dress I wore to my first festival — the solstice at Stonehenge in 1989." (Fraggle)

Red and black hat, cotton velvet and denim, Susie Franks; cotton and Lycra dress; cotton bedshirt; cotton T-shirt, Company, France; cotton vest; cotton and wool, embroidered waistcoat, India; cotton and Lycra leggings, Blue Pacific; cotton patched leggings; hand-made acrylic socks; woollen legwarmers; leather para boots; multicoloured laces; wooden spoon, ocarina, wooden crochet hooks, liquorice stick, velvet pouch, all made by Fraggle

Traveller UK 1986-94

Green and yellow cotton, tie-dyed
Donga hat; cotton T-shirt,
Army Surplus; hand-knitted wool
Jumper, South America; denim jeans;
leather belt; leather Para boots;
liquorice sticks; penny whistle;
toggle; bracelet; woollen sacks

This male Traveller outfit combines second-hand
clothing, army surplus and handmade garments.
Numerous layers are worn for warmth and protection—
the hat is specific to the Donga tribe. The clothes
are threadbare because they are usually worn
until they fall apart, and their unwashed
appearance is the result of an itinerant life spent outdoors

Worn by a member of the Donga tribe.

Fashion New Age Travellers
Michiko Koshino - UK, Autumn/Winter 1993.
Blue wool hat, cotton blouse, wool waistcoat,
tweed skirt with leather belt, patchwork
work leggings, scarf, gloves, tweed and leather sho

The heavy duty, economical and customized clothes
of New Age Travellers acted as the springboard
for this ensemble. 'I have reworked the recessionary
chic of the New age Traveller to create new, funky
street and club wear' (Michiko Koshino)
Given by Michiko Koshino

Traveller
UK 1994
Rainbow cotton
crocheted hat &
woollen patchwork
poncho; cotton
T-shirt, Bhs;
acrylic Knitted
tights; cotton and
polyester skirt;
Sheepskin booties

Members of the Donga Tribe
helped Fraggle assemble this baby's
outfit by contributing tiny garments
which they had aquired at different
times and various sources. Their budget
is limited and new clothes are not
central to their existence, so, in
a time-honoured tradition,
clothes are passed down from brothers
and sisters. Babies are often given gifts
of handmade garments. Elements such
as the patchwork poncho and rainbow
hat mirror the style of adult travellers

hat lent by Florence Orme
Compiled by Fraggle

ECO

Cream patchwork wool hat,
jacket, top and skirt,
CONSCIOUS EARTHWEAR;
leather sandals, BIRKENSTOCKS,
Germany; wood, bone and
beaded necklace, CHRIS MORRISON

UK 1993

Sarah Ratty began designing T-shirts
with David Jenkins in the late 1980s.
Many of these were worn by Ravers
and New Age Travellers. By 1990
she had begun to design clothes
which were recycled from old jumpers,
under the company name of Conscious
Earthwear. In 1994-5 she introduced
recycled, ecologically sound clothing
to the top end of the fashion
market, selling her designs in
Harrods and Browns.

FASHION ECO
LYALL HAKARAIA
UK SPRING/SUMMER 1993

Raffia cape, dip-dyed indigo silk
jersey dress, raffia, shell and amber
necklace, recycled shoes with raffia and
shell uppers 'I want to use all organic
products to produce clothes that are
innovative, fashionable and wearable'
(Lyall Hakaraia).Given by Lyall Hakaraia

UK 1991-4

Red cotton recycled jacket,
EGGPLANT; cotton T-shirt; recycled
patch trousers, KILLOGRAM; vegetarian
Dr Martens, VEGETARIAN SHOES
'I collect old fabrics and cut-offs
and piece them back together to make
something new. Its called making good use
of the things that we find' (Graham Evans).
Boots given by Vegetarian Shoes
T-shirt lent by Stephen King

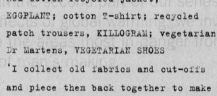

RAVERS/'MADCHESTER'
UK 1987-8

Green and white cotton T-shirt, Big Banana;
tie-dyed cotton T-shirt, Have a Nice Day;
denim flares, Joe Bloggs; leather boots,
Kickers France

The Northern Rave scene was centred in
and around Manchester and Liverpool. Its
young exponents steered away from the
football terraces and into clubs like the
Hacienda. They created their own cheeky,
androgynous and baggy style which
featured amusing T-shirts printed with puns
on weel-known trademarks. Manchester
clothing companies, such as Joe Bloggs,
became synonymous with this style.

T-shirt given by Simon Debenham
Jeans given by Joe Bloggs
Shoes given by Kickers

wild green

RAVERS
ACID RAVE

1986-88

RAVERS/ACID RAVE UK 1986

Black and yellow Smiley cotton T-shirt; cotton T-shirt, Shoom; printed cotton shorts, Mambo, Australia; leather trainers, Travel Fox; bandanna.

Sun, sea and surf with a twist of Chicago House music and acid were the inspiration behind the Mediterranean club scene particular to Ibiza in the mid-1980s. In order to recreate the holiday atmosphere in the London clubs, a mixture of leisure and activity wear including brightly coloured baggy surf clothes lent themselves to frantic, non-stop, all-night dancing.

Shorts given by Neil Harvey Smiley T-shirt lent by Stuart Harrison Shoom T-shirts and Travel Fox trainers given by Fiona Cartledge

RAVERS

FASHION RAVE

1989-94

**FASHION RAVE MOSCHINO
ITALY 1994**

Printed cotton T-shirt 'No To Racism' Hippies first used
the Smiley face design to signify their enjoyment of
hallucinogenic drugs, and it was revived in the late 1980s
by members of the Rave scene. It also became the
signature motif of rebel Italian designer Franco Moschino.
This T-shirt is one of a series he designed, which used the
Smiley face in conjunction with political slogans.

Given by Moschino

RAVERS UK 1989-90

Red quilted nylon jacket, Naf Naf, France; cotton T-shirt and cotton and polyester hooded sweatshirt, Conscious Earthwear; denim dungarees, Dickies; suede Wallabies, Spain

While retaining stylistic aspects of earlier versions of this subculture - baggy dungarees (1988) and Acid House orange Wallabies (1986) - the Ravers continally updated their style by adding garments such as the New Age T-shirt and the Euro-Casual jacket. These components formed an eminently sensible outfit for dancing all night in a field. By 1990 the Rave scene had begun to fragment into a myriad of looks, as was manifest in contemporary streetstyle.

Jacket given by Naf Naf
T-shirt lent by Sarah Ratty and
David Jenkins, Conscious Earthwear
Sweatshirt given by Sarah Ratty
and David Jenkins, Conscious Earthwear

FASHION RAVE RIFAT OZBEK
UK SPRING/SUMMER 1990

White quilted synthetic jacket, synthetic top with glass beads, synthetic shorts; customized Converse 2000 trainers; rope and silver necklace, S-Tek. 1990
'Ecstasy - Enlightenment - Purity - New Age' (Rifat Ozbek).

Necklace given by Stephen King, S-Tek
Shorts and top worn and given by Lucy Ferry
Jacket and customized trainers given by Rifat Ozbek

GRUNGE

brOWN

wool tWeed ... Given by donna Kayam ...

1988-90

GRuNGe

reD and BlAck HaND-knitted acrylic jumPer;
cOtton T-shirt, conflict; denim jeans;

Levi'S, uSa; woOllen plaid shiRt;

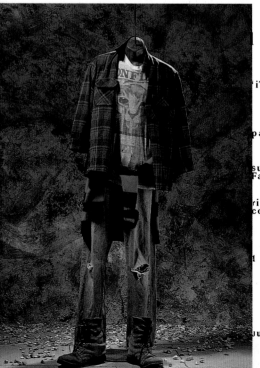

leather boots, army surplus

'iT CouLD be AmerICA's mOSt sicnIficant wHjte yoUTH culture
in 25 years' (the Face, AUgust 1992).

parallelinG bRItish iNDie, American GruncE eNcompasseS

seconD-Hand cloTHinG and inCorporaTes eLEmenTs oF SkaTe,
surF anD thrash metAl STyles. representTInG a bRItish Variant, a
Favourite Punk T-shirt and jumper jOin a GRuncy shirt AND

ripped jeanS. Like punk, tHe mOVEment wAS anTi-fashion - a
complete   antithesis   tO   the

mainLinE power dressinG of the
1980s.   dONnA

shirt and JEANS Given by SHAun turPin
jumper, t-Shirt aND Boots worn aND GiveN by MArk hEWSON

FASdurioNnGe

USaSPrinG/summer 1993

brown wool tWeed jacket, Felt and LeAther cap,
ribb Ed cotton TOp, wool
waistcoat, Fair Isle cardiGan, WOol cardiGan,
prINted crêpe skirt, cotton leGGinGs, cotton sOCks, wool sockS;
leather boots, maTterhorN for dkNY

'i'm forever Inspired by the s t r e e t
style of new yOrK city and h o w y o u n G , hip
PeoPle instInCTive ly pull themselves toGether.

This look has a natural, just thrown
toGether feelinG tHaT's aLL about spirit,
attitude and individuality' (donNA KAran).

GivEn bY d o N N a K A r a n

(^dKnY) KARan

uk Bhangra

green synthetic shirt;
suede waistcoat,
Nickelbys; cotton trousers.

Anjum Sheik lives in Leicester and spends many of his
evenings at the local Bhangra nightclub. On a Bhangra
DJ night he wears B-Boy style jeans, T-shirt and trainers.
However when a Bhangra band is playing live, he
smartens up his attire and wears this outfit. The shirt was
made with a Nehru collar by an Indian tailor in
Leicester (£15 material, £10 labour) and the trousers
were bought for £20 from the local market. He wore
these with fine leather slip-on shoes and African copper
jewellery. Worn by Anjum Sheik

Multicoloured patch-
work wool hat,
Catweasle; cotton
and Lycra body,
Next; cotton T-shirt;
cotton and Lycra
vest; acrylic and
cotton cardigan,
Warehouse; cotton
knit leggings;
denim cut-offs,
Traffic; leather and
metal belt; suede
ankle boots. College

Subcultural Style 1993–4

Blue denim jeans,
Levi's, USA; cotton
T-shirt, Aantoni &
Alison; nylon dress,
Top Shop; mohair
jumper, Angela Salt;
ex-army cotton
parka; leather hik-
ing boots; Captain
America pendant;
Elvis in Las Vegas
sun-glasses;
Walkman, Snoy;
patriotic lolly, Astro
This eclectic outfit
was worn by
Angela Salt to
Techno / Ambient
parties and clubs
throughout 1994.
It is a mixture of
accessible high
street garments,
combined with army
surplus to give an
almost futuristic
look known as New
Age-Ambient-Techno.
Worn by Angela Salt

An outfit reflecting a
number of earlier
subcultural styles;
the tie-dye stems
from Hippies, the
layering effect from
Travellers, the loose
fit from Rave while
the jewellery adds a
note of ethnicity. Out
of necessity,
Travellers re-cycle
clothing but here
new, chainstore
merchandise is mixed
with customized
garments to achieve
the desired look.
Worn by Hannah Crib

Fashion Subcultural Style

Black, white and mauve knitted cotton and Lurex hat, synthetic ciré jacket, knitted cotton and lurex tank-top and shorts, leather bag and studded collar, leather shoes with wood soles, belt, spangle stockings, The Peruvian Connection for Anna Sui

Anna Sui's distinctive, eclectic, approach to fashion reflects an interest in ethnicity, 1970s revivalism and futuristic Cyber looks. These are areas stylistically represented in subcultural style in the mid 1990s. Given by Anna Sui

Anna Sui USA Spring/Summer 1994

Jungle
Ragga
94

RAGGA UK 1994

**Black satin and tulle bra top with gold
metal button decoration, gold metal
jewellery, quilted satin zipped chaps,
stretch tulle shorts, Pascale for Against
All Oz; quilted satin bag, Philippines;
leather shoes, Office Shoes**

**'We wanted a kind of Cowboy look so we
made the chaps and carried the dance
hall style through with gold buttons. Girls
were wearing things like Wonderbras so
we decided to make it in Chanel-style**

RAGGA UK 1984-92

White denim shirt, 1984, denim jeans, 1992, Exhaust; leather boots, Grinders, 1993

Danny Edwards wore these garments as an outfit in 1992. He acquired the shirt from his uncle's shop Stars in Dalston in 1984. The jeans, although made by the same company, Exhaust, and a favourite label with Ragga-muffins, were bought whilst he was in Kingston, Jamaica, in 1992. The boots came from Camden Town in 1993.

Worn by Danny Edwards

Jungle
Ragga
84-94

RAGGA UK 1994

Pink linen and sheer polyester suit with gold braid, Andrew Dunbar; velvet, plastic and jewelled shoes, Sabiba

Andrew Dunbar is a Jamaican designer based in London. His use of brilliant colour and gold and sheer fabrics is a classic Ragga feature. This suit is flamboyant and revealing without hugging the body.

RAGGA UK 1994

Purple/orange two-tone crushed velvet jacket, with gold braid trim, black/red two-tone crushed velvet trousers, Against All OZ; leather shoes, Bally

'I made one for myself and then everyone kept asking about it and I ended up making ten more. It's for the evening - I'd wear it to a blues or a dance, but I have worn it during the day, when I've rolled up the trousers, tucked in the shirt and worn it with trainers. In the evening I'd wear it with a pair of Italian cut shoes' (Oz).

Worn by Oz

JUNGLE UK 1994

White cotton T-shirt, leather belt, Moschino, Italy; denim jeans, Armani, Italy

The style that is worn to Jungle clubs like Thunder and Joy is very designer-oriented. It reflects many styles from the past including Ragga, Casual, Rave and B-Boy.

'Jungle people wear straight jeans, not baggy or bleached. I wear labels like Moschino, Armani and Ralph Lauren because they are casual but designer' (Anonymous Junglist)

* Screen Cyberpunk
  Jean Paul Gaultier:
  ▯••▯▯*•▯▯*

  >Green silk grosgrain
   zipped jacket with metal,
   electrical wire details
   and detatchable pockets;
   bra with headlight cups;
   leather holster;
   zipped leggings;
   padded stretch girdle;
   leather and elastic
   fingerless gloves;
   canvas ankle boots;
   ring, earrings and beads.
      ••   *• *

  >given by

  >and

>France
>1994

>Jean Paul Gaultier

>Pedro Almodovar
>*
>▯▯

>Worn by Victoria
 Abril who plays
 Andrea 'Scarface'
 Caracortada in
 Pedro Almodovar's
 cult film 'Kika'.
 Scarface is
 featured roaming
 Madrid on her
 motorbike wearing
 these futuristic,
 electronically
 operated combat
 clothes. Jean
 Paul Gaultier
 was invited to
 design the
 costumes with
 input from
 director Pedro
 Almodovar.

>

     ▯▯*•

*Cyberpunk: >UK
                 >1991

>Black neoprene,
 silver metal and
 moulded plastic body,
 armpiece,
 neoprene and suynthetic
 fibre gloves,
 metal hydraulic and
 pneumatic handpieces,
 rubber knee guards,
 rubber and neoprene boots.

>□□*

>Ryo Inoue,
 Japan.
>*
>*

>"The title of this
 collection was Cybernetic
 Collection (a fusion
 of the human body,
 technology and media).
 The message I wanted to
 deliver was that of the
 human body as a part of
 media/information and
 also to question the
 environment which surrounds
 us by laying technology
 close to the body.
 The final outcome was a
 collection, eclectic in
 concept, in which I was
 to interpret the movemnet
 of human joints and
 muscles with metal".

>(Ryo Inoue).

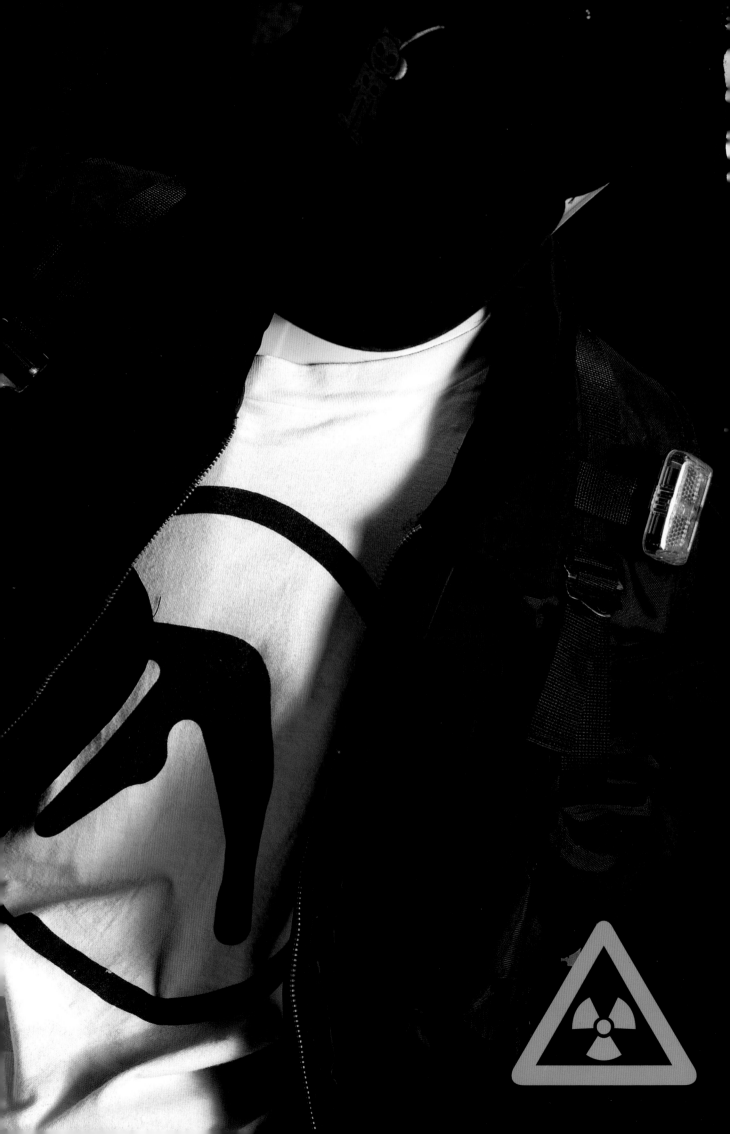

Techno.UK.1992/3

Black nylon MA1 flight jacket [USA]
Baseball hat [Timex Posse]
Nylon combat vest with Rave light
cotton T-shirt [Aphex Twin]
Cotton jeans [G-force]
Leather trainers [Converse High Tops USA]
Metal dog tag

Techno can be split into two major groups - Ambient and Hard Core Techno. The later is dominated by a fast drum beat and is characterized by militaristic and aggressive garments. The style brings together elements of dress from B-Boys, Skaters and Rave mixed with army surplus. Combat gear has the added advantage of numerous pockets for cash, drugs and water bottles.

Worn by Stuart Harrison
Trainers and vest lent by Stuart Harrison
Jeans lent by Cathie Dingwall

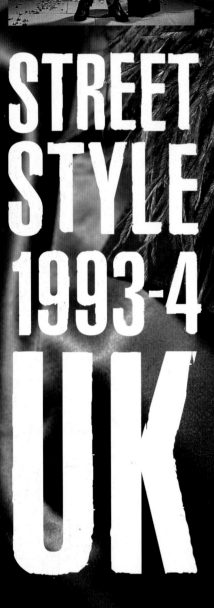

STREET
STYLE
1993-4
UK

BLUE SATIN JACKET AND TROUSERS, CHIFFON AND OSTRICH FEATHER BLOUSE, HAMMISH MORROW; SHOES, OFFICE

SHOES. INFLUENCES: GLAM, TEDDY BOY, FUNK. SUIT GIVEN BY HAMMISH MORROW. SHOES GIVEN BY OFFICE SHOES

BLACK LEATHER JACKET, COTTON PLAID SHIRT, STUSSY, USA; DENIM JEANS, LEVI'S, USA; GREEN WOOL

BERET, KANGOL; LOAFERS, PATRICK COX; BEADS. INFLUENCES: ACID JAZZ B-BOYS, BEATNIK, BIKER.

JACKET AND SHIRT GIVEN BY STUSSY. LOAFERS GIVEN BY PATRICK COX.   BERET GIVEN BY KANGOL

MULTI-COLOURED WOOLLEN JUMPER, AMANO, BOLIVIA; BARK AND SHELL WAISTCOAT, AND BAG, KOMODO; DENIM

FLARED JEANS, LEVI'S, USA, 1970S; WOOLLEN SOCKS; LEATHER AND CORK SANDALS, BIRKENSTOCK, GERMANY

INFLUENCES: SOUTH AMERICAN, HIPPIE, FOLKIES. WAISTCOAT GIVEN BY KOMODO JEANS GIVEN BY TRUDY BARBER

RED NYLON DRESS, LEATHER BOOTS, MURRAY AND VERN. INFLUENCES: FETISH, PUNK, GOTH, COMPILED BY MURRAY AND VERN

BLACK-AND-WHITE FAKE HORSESKIN WAISTCOAT AND JEANS, PAUL TUNSTALL; COTTON T-SHIRT, ANTONI AND ALISON; BOOTS, OFFICE SHOES; SILVER PENDANT, S-TEK

INFLUENCES: WESTERN, NATIVE AMERICAN, WORKWEAR, BIKERS, GAY STYLES. TROUSERS AND WAISTCOAT GIVEN BY PAUL TUNSTALL. BOOTS GIVEN BY OFFICE SHOES

SHEEPSKIN WAISTCOAT, DENIM MINISKIRT AND CORSET TOP, BIONIC; LEATHER BOOTS, DINGO INFLUENCES: WESTERN, WORKWEAR, FETISH, SKINHEADS. COMPILED BY CLARE TRANTER

COTTON AND LYCRA BODY SUIT · PAM HOGG, TRAINERS, FILA; PENDANT, S·TEK. INFLUENCES: RAGGA, CYBERPUNK, FETISH. COMPILED BY PAM HOGG

BROWN, GREEN AND CREAM STRIPED COTTON TWILL JEANS, KOMODO; WOOLLEN WAISTCOAT; CROCHET WOOL CLOCHE; TRAINERS, ADIDAS

GAZELLES, GERMANY; POMEGRANATE SEED NECKLACE. INFLUENCES: ACID JAZZ, BEATNIK, HIPPY, OLD SKOOL, RAVE. WORN BY EMMA GOODMAN

ORANGE NYLON JACKET, COTTON TRACKPANTS, COTTON T-SHIRT, DANIEL POOLE; LEATHER BOOTS, CATERPILLAR, USA; SILVER NECKLACE, S·TEK. INFLUENCES:

CYBERPUNK, HIP HOP, TECHNO, AFRICAN ETHNIC. JACKET, TRACKPANTS AND T-SHIRT GIVEN BY DANIEL POOLE. CATERPILLARS GIVEN BY OFFICE SHOES

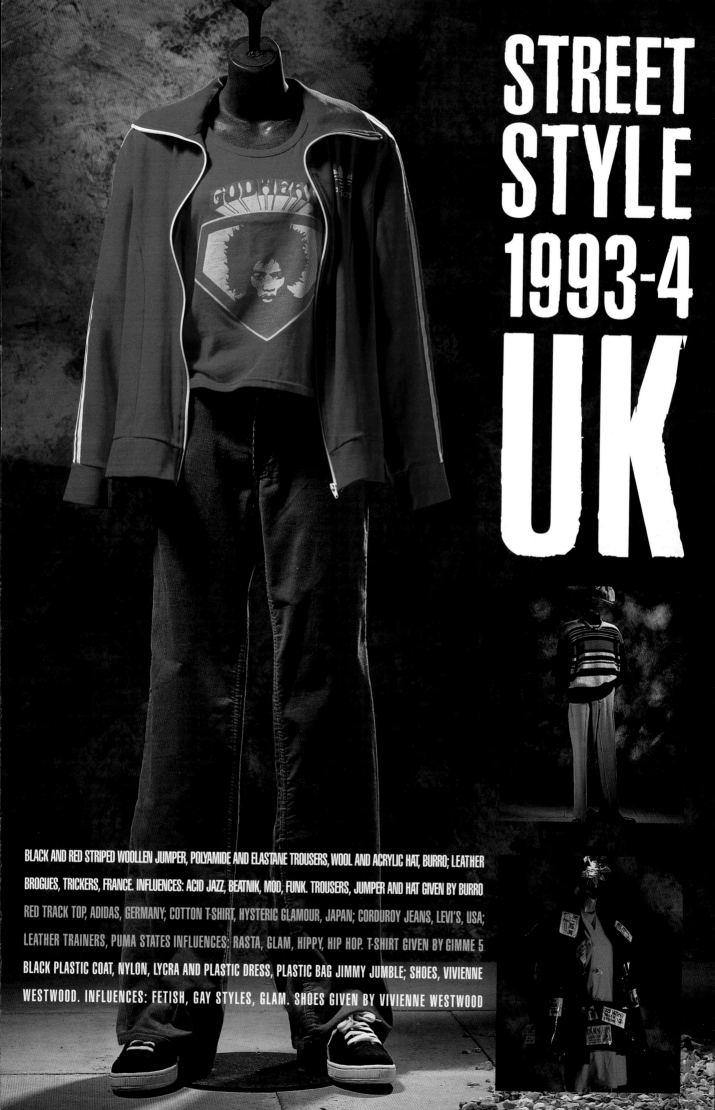

STREET STYLE 1993-4 UK

BLACK AND RED STRIPED WOOLLEN JUMPER, POLYAMIDE AND ELASTANE TROUSERS, WOOL AND ACRYLIC HAT, BURRO; LEATHER BROGUES, TRICKERS, FRANCE. INFLUENCES: ACID JAZZ, BEATNIK, MOD, FUNK. TROUSERS, JUMPER AND HAT GIVEN BY BURRO

RED TRACK TOP, ADIDAS, GERMANY; COTTON T-SHIRT, HYSTERIC GLAMOUR, JAPAN; CORDUROY JEANS, LEVI'S, USA; LEATHER TRAINERS, PUMA STATES INFLUENCES: RASTA, GLAM, HIPPY, HIP HOP. T-SHIRT GIVEN BY GIMME 5

BLACK PLASTIC COAT, NYLON, LYCRA AND PLASTIC DRESS, PLASTIC BAG JIMMY JUMBLE; SHOES, VIVIENNE WESTWOOD. INFLUENCES: FETISH, GAY STYLES, GLAM. SHOES GIVEN BY VIVIENNE WESTWOOD

Future Street Style
uk/2045 [1994]

Reflective sleeveless top and mini-wrap skirt RYO INOUE 1994 • chenille and Lycra knit sleeves CAROLYN RANDOLFI 1993 • cotton jersey bonnet THE ORIGINAL FIFI LAMBSHTRUMPH 1994 • optical cross ANELA TAKAC with central rotating element by IAN READER 1994 • technology gloves HENRIETTE JANDER 1994 • modem boots JOHNNY MOKE 1994

'Corporate companies could employ people to wear symbols of their organization, as computer systems become more wearable • Clothes are lightweight yet hardwearing, containing devices to read credit cards [WITH FINGER SCANNERS] • digital displays on breast panels • instruments to produce 3-D holograms, all to service the public's constant demand for immediate information' [GAVIN FERNANDES]

Compiled by GAVIN FERNANDES

Blue hooded utility jacket MICHAEL UDO 1992 • synthetic trousers REBECCA EARLEY 1994 • neoprene and rubber shoes RYO INOUE 1994 • plastic, neoprene and metal bag PETER HITCHCOCK 1994 • blue cotton gloves · Combining the elements of protection with the aesthetics of sportswear, the second-skin jacket is made from a high-performance sandwiched fabric • The trousers can be self-styled by reshaping the fabric around the legs • The gloves form a visual deterrent and the bag is ergonomically designed to prevent perspiration forming on the back [GAVIN FERNANDEZ] Bag lent by PETER HITCHCOCK • Jacket lent by MICHAEL UDO • Shoes lent by RYO INOUE • Compiled by GAVIN FERNANDES

Future Street Style
uk/2045 [1994]

Green knitted dress CAROLYN RANDOLFI 1992 • synthetic waistcoat ELEY-KISHIMOTO 1994 • leather jacket CRAIG MORISSON 1994 • leggings and shoes JOHANNE PRICE and ANDREW BUCKLER 1993 • choker and neck-lace MIKE TURNER 1994 • copper and lens bag PATRICK BULLOCK 1994

For future travellers in the year 2045, certain clothing could be made up of artificial, bio-genetically grown skins and fur [I.E. GROWN INDUSTRIALLY IN VATS RATHER THAN OBTAINED FROM A SLAUGHTERED ANIMAL] • Some skins can be genetically mixed, for example the look of a crocodile texture with the feel of pigskin • Copper bags carry plants and remedies which are sold to people in cities' [GAVIN FERNANDES] •
Compiled by GAVIN FERNANDES

Brown leather jacket ANELA TAKAC 1993 • coin vest REBECCA EARLEY 1994 • embossed leather skirt ALISON HEYHOE 1994 • synthetic trousers CHARLIE HUNTER 1994 • shoes MICHELLE STEWART 1994 • skull necklace PIRATE RIK 1994 • belt, headpiece, copper casket and necklace MICHELLE FERNANDES 1994 • eyewear STEVEN JARVIS 1994

'In the year 2045, the Traveller population has grown so large they have become the new indigenous tribe of Britain, wearing a combination of second-hand surplus with self-made clothes and jewellery made from recycled vintage copper and silver coins • Certain tribes sell rare homeopathic plants and remedies which are carried in distinctive copper neck caskets' [GAVIN FERNANDES] •
Compiled by GAVIN FERNANDES

CONCLUSION

The response to the Streetstyle Exhibition was phenomenal. In terms of attendances, visitor numbers exceeded the projected 70,000, reaching a staggering 109,000 in just under fourteen weeks. Media coverage was overwhelming, amounting to some £2 million of free worldwide, and broad-ranging, television, magazine and newspaper articles. There was also a pro-active education programme, which successfully served to disseminate information to specialist as well as general audiences.

On the whole, the response was very positive. It was acknowledged that in assembling the exhibition, curators and researchers had gone beyond the realms of traditional V&A acquisition. The Monsters of Rock Festival at Castle Donnington yielded insights into heavy metal culture; Glastonbury Festival was the hunting ground for New Age Traveller clothes, and clubs in London, Manchester and Bristol also proved invaluable for making contacts and identifying sources of clothing. The momentum of organizing a high profile exhibition made acquiring clothing and primary research undoubtedly easier. The V&A now has a unique collection of subcultural clothing, with complementary high fashion spin-offs, which has enriched the national collection of dress and broadened its appeal.

Inevitably, criticisms were made, many valid and constructive. We are pleased with, but also modest about, the results of the exhibition. It was an ambitious project, charting newer territory than was offered as a starting point. As a result, our own researches have continued to assess and question the validity of our approach. Interesting views and perspectives are still being debated by theorists in the fields of museology, design, dress and cultural studies. With the aid of a grant from the V&A's Research Department, it was possible to formalize these debates in a series of interviews conducted after the exhibition, culminating in a symposium. This chapter summarizes some of the issues raised.

Do the clothes collected for the exhibition give insight into the past?

'I was a Punk (B-Boy, Skater, Beatnik) but I didn't wear that.'

This was the most frequently overheard comment from visitors at the exhibition. The concern was that the clothes exhibited were not identical to those visitors had worn or seen themselves. Clothes are so personal and accessible (especially those from the 20th century) that in an exhibition of this kind, where only one or two examples of a particular group are shown, they cannot and did not attempt to be representative. As stated in the first chapter, the clothes are representational of the people who wore them. Sadly, some visitors left the exhibition not having realized that the clothes were 'authentic', in spite of didactic information stating who had worn the outfits and when. Removing the clothes from their cultural contexts is clearly problematic. This was reinforced by a critic who wrote that, 'seeing the clothes was like meeting a famous film star you had idolised for years, disappointing' (Peter York, *The Times*, November 1994).

Wherever possible, to put 'flesh and blood' into the clothes, we used oral evidence in the form of direct quotations in the labels to let individuals give expression to the clothes and the periods. For example, Steve Pang, B-Boy during the 1980s, said in an interview:

'I was fourteen and living in Bristol when I first became interested in being a B-Boy. I was watching kids rapping but they were confused because they were wearing Casual clothes and rapping to hip-hop. I was getting into clothes because of the labels. Then I accidentally bought the soundtrack to Wildstyle and that was really the start of it. Everyone wanted Kangol hats – no matter how stupid they looked, and Puma States. Basically, it was much more credible if you couldn't buy it off the shelf.' (Steve Pang, interviewed for the *Independent* by Sarah Callard, November 1994).

It is the very individual nature of subcultural dress that would have prompted this response. Variations in style, such as regional differences, were often misinterpreted by visitors as a sign of inaccuracy.

Despite the problems of putting together such a controversial exhibition, we hope that the outcome was a deeper understanding of the 'relationship between people and things'. What has become apparent, as Daniel Miller (anthropologist at University College, London) in his book *Material Culture and Mass Consumption* indicates, is that when isolating 'trivial' objects and 'holding them up for academic scrutiny', the outcome can be perilous and contentious. We collected the clothes to reflect and document some of the major subcultural style groups since the early 1940s. We wished to explore how present styles are created from the past – a trend which has been highlighted by debates on Postmodernism. As Susan M. Pearce (lecturer on the Leicester Museums MA course) states in her book *Interpreting Objects and Collections*, 'both objects and collections can and should be studied in their own right, as part of the broader pattern of cultural studies'.

What we can see from analysing the diverse reactions to this exhibition is the contradiction between the general and particular experience of individuals. Objects convey different messages to different people depending on the individual's original experience of those items that he or she is viewing.

Should museums display such outfits out of their cultural context?

This question was prompted by a statement by Michael Horsham (senior lecturer at Camberwell School of Art and freelance design writer) in an interview:

'I think if there was one major fault with the whole exhibition it was the steadfast refusal to engage with any political dimension, in any real sense. The whole context is about trying to flesh out objects, trying to make them make sense in terms of the real world. Having said that, I'm not quite sure how it could have been achieved in any kind of realistic way without setting the institution up for criticism.'

Museum approaches vary. Social history collections often demand a different viewpoint from that of art and design institutions. Re-creating the total environment and producing a Jorvik Centre style exhibition involves a different policy from that of a decorative arts museum, such as the V&A, which tends to focus upon the object *per se* and then on its dynamic relationship to similar objects, augmented with contextual written information.

The Streetstyle Exhibition was diverse, as each of the subcultures has a distinctive environment. It would have been almost impossible, extremely expensive and, to us, inappropriate, to attempt to re-create them all. The aim was to present a new object-based analysis of clothing, which is the most visible emblem of subcultural identity. By presenting visitors with tangible objects belonging to their history, museums can go some way towards providing a key to past as well as present circumstances. What was successfully achieved was highlighted by Mark Suggitt, of the Yorkshire and Humberside Museums Council, who wrote, 'Any show which tries to communicate the ragbag of emotion and angst of youth through the medium of objects is going to have a hard time. Streetstyle wisely homes in on the most visual aspect of the conscious dissidence of youth – clothes'.

Do the confines of an exhibition mean the subject may become sanitized?

In a sense sanitization was inevitable, given the constraints of space allocated to each subculture – over 50 were represented in two galleries. The breadth of the subject meant that it was imperative to set specific criteria. In deciding how we would approach our task we first reflected on a working definition of youth subculture. Stuart Hall (Open University) in his book *Resistance Through Rituals* states: 'Subcultures must exhibit a distinctive enough shape and structure to make them different from their parent culture. They must be focused around certain activities, values, certain uses of material artifacts, territorial spaces etc.'

Using this definition, we were able to enquire whether the identified subcultures had or have recognizable styles. Furthermore we were reluctant to narrow down our selection of outfits on the basis of ideological concerns. To leave out a subculture with a rich stylistic history because of political considerations was problematic. We also had to consider how the donors of objects felt about the way they would be represented. Skinheads, for example, were adamant that they should not be portrayed as fascist and racist thugs.

Is personal experience detrimental to the formation of an unbiased approach?

To explore this question it is necessary to view it historically. From the 18th century, the rule of religion began to be questioned, 'knowledge' became separated and classified under the specific subjects of science, morality and art. These in turn were categorized: Science was held to be the truth, Morality equalled what was 'right', and Art meant authenticity and beauty. As each field expanded it became institutionalized. Jurgen Habermas, cultural philosopher, terms this historical compartmentalization 'the project of modernity' (in a book by Hal Foster, *PostModern Culture*). He goes on to state: 'each domain of culture could be made to correspond to cultural professions in which problems could be dealt with as the concern of special experts'.

In attempting to approach a subject with some degree of impartiality it is necessary to step back from the project in hand, and achieving a balanced view on a subject is obviously challenging.

While working on the exhibition, we acquired a broad-based knowledge, covering many decades of subcultures and drawing on a variety of sources. We also had to become impartial arbitrators between many personal and specific views given by individuals who were immersed in their own subculture. On one level, our personal experiences of subcultural groups were advantageous. However, as the project developed, we became wary that these could influence our approach to the subject. The diversity encountered amongst subcultural groups underlined the specificity of any experience we may have had personally.

Habermas's 'project of modernity' explains historically why it was necessary to rationalize our experience and knowledge, but taking into account the increasing complexity of late 20th-century society and the nature of subcultural dress, his explanation is an idealized one.

It is precisely the personal element that may in this case deflect the criticism levelled by the originators of the subject, the people who wore the outfits. The perceived nature of large art institutions can lead to the assumption that a true understanding or appreciation of the subtleties of the subject may never be achieved. By categorizing and pigeonholing subcultural dress without the benefit of personal insight there is a danger that, as Habermas expounds, 'the distance grows between the culture of the experts and that of the larger public'.

The question of balance thus becomes important because it is difficult for us not to have had personal experience in some shape or form with late 20th-century dress.

Can museums only be a tool of dominant ideology?

The V&A is a mainstream British cultural institution. By collecting subcultural dress, the Museum is contributing to the more general acceptance in society of such ways of dressing. One of the fundamental reasons for wearing subcultural clothes was, and is, that they are a visual expression of nonconformity. Thus the Museum could be criticized for institutionalizing an act of rebellion, such as the Punk or Rocker dressing in a way that seeks to intimidate.

To explore this at its simplest level, the traditional Left sees the increase in diversity in today's society as breaking up the core of working-class cultural identity. It sees oppression inevitably as the end product of this change and affirms the Marxist theory which would firmly place museums alongside a wide variety of exploitative and oppressive institutions and regards them as a tool of the dominant ideology. The traditional Right has similar fears, but for different reasons, namely a concern that society is suffering a loss of traditional 'high' cultural attitudes and status, a fear that has been expressed in art institutions like the V&A. The result of this fear is that the Right no longer sees museums as a tool of the dominant ideology.

Both the Left and Right experience a crisis of confidence with the shifting boundaries of the old class system and the homogenization of culture, anxieties that have been compounded by the all-pervasive influence of popular culture, especially American. Both arguments subscribe to certain blanket assumptions concerning the negative consequences of the growth of popular culture. These negative critiques of the last few decades have produced what is termed 'retrospective regret', a heightened perception of the past as being better than the present.

However, there is an alternative interpretation of popular culture, and it is possible to see the social, economic and cultural changes over the last century leading to positive possibilities. The processes of reinterpretation, modification and acceptance of previously unacceptable elements are the dynamics of change in our Western material culture. These are changes that have occurred in the last 40 years in society in general and also, therefore, in the ways museums exhibit and the impact of such exhibits. The growth and acceptance of popular culture have increased understanding and interest in the past, and thus in turn have fuelled the growing popularity of museums worldwide. As a result museums, once the sole preserve of the upper middle classes, have been able to change with society as a whole. Thus we have the Streetstyle Exhibition. The visiting public's expectations are changing the attitudes of the large art institutions, who are having to adapt. The positive fluidity of contemporary culture is reflected in postmodern ideas, which in turn are expressed by institutions such as the V&A.

By representing varied 'cultural levels', such as concepts of 'high' and 'low' culture in museums, it is to be hoped that the danger of reflecting the dominant ideology will be bypassed.

Youth culture has been widely publicized, but few people have understood its significance as one of the most striking and visible manifestations of social and political change in post-war Britain. We hope the Collection, and this book, go some way towards expressing the significance of this phenomenon.

By staging the exhibition it has been suggested that we have signalled the death of subcultures. It is sad that the media should only associate museums with historical objects and not recognize that they actively face the hard challenge of collecting what is here and now as well. Our role as museum curators is to collect, preserve and make accessible. What the Streetstyle Exhibition achieved was to set in motion this process; it was a starting point, not the final word. Michael Horsham encapsulated the point of the exhibition in an article he wrote for *Arena* magazine in November 1994:

'...place the spookily ordinary customised punk outfit from 1976 next to the punk-inspired creations of Versace et al and the point of the exhibition becomes clear. In the modern world which has been developing since World War Two, the cultural map is turned upside down, couture looks to the street and vice versa. If the exhibition can provoke comment and memory along those lines then good on the V&A I say.'

BIBLIOGRAPHY

Daniel Miller, *Material Culture and Mass Consumption* (Blackwell, 1987)

Susan M. Pearce, *Interpreting Objects and Collections* (Routledge, 1994)

Stuart Hall, *Resistance Through Rituals* (Routledge, 1975)

Hal Foster, *Post Modern Culture* (Pluto Press, 1990)

THANKS

We extend thanks to Shaun Cole, Sarah Callard, Maxine Smitheram, Judy Westacott, Debbie Sinfield, Gavin Fernandes, Carol Tulloch, Will Hoon, Steve Pang, Stuart Harrison, Derek and Esther Falconer of Crazy Clothes, Jo Wallace, Cherry Parker, John Stuart, Normski, John Simon, Mike Ferrante, Philip Sallon, Lou Taylor, Elizabeth Wilson, Sally Merriman, John Hardy, Kevin Reitze, Sue Milner, Sue Snell, Marion Hume, Tony Glenville, Ruo Inoue, Justin Alphonse, Andy at Slam City Skates, Simon Debenham, Olie Fitzgerald and Tim Ranger at Low Pressure, John and Molly Dove of Modzart, Fiona Cartledge of Sign of the Times, Keith Mallinson, Katrina Beatty, Morticia, Chris Sullivan, Chris Moore and to the many others who offered support and guidance.

We are indebted to the donors, who are individually credited in the captions. We are most grateful to them for parting with cherished clothing to help build a unique collection. We also thank those who lent items both for the exhibition and to be photographed for the book.

Amy de la Haye, co-author of the highly successful *Chanel, the Couturière at Work,* and Cathie Dingwall are curators working on 20th-Century dress at the Victoria and Albert Museum. The photographs which were specially taken for this book are by Daniel McGrath.

Creating Graphics, books and identities for many well-known companies, the designers of this book – johnson banks – also designed the graphic identity for the V&A's William Morris Centenary Exhibition.

Any similarities between the graphic styles created in this book and those of other graphic designers of the last fifty years are entirely intentional.